Volume 19, Number 2

differences

In the Event: An Introduction

If it keeps on rainin',
   levee's goin' to break
If it keeps on rainin',
   levee's goin' to break
And all these people have no place to
stay.
—Memphis Minnie

Obviously, if there is an event, it must
never be something that is predicted or
planned, or even really decided upon.
—Derrida

Constructive criticism for Plantation
lords.
watch out.
—Walker

*I*n the weeks immediately following Hurricane Katrina's landfall, the enemies were clear and easy to name. Or so it seemed to New
Orleanians. Dispersed across the region and the nation, the city's displaced
residents labored through their distraction to construct a roll call of the
dishonorable and the blameworthy. In online forums, television interviews, and phone calls to family, they identified the agents of destruction by
name: "Dubya," "Dick," FEMA, the Levee Board, "Brownie," Blanco, Nagin,
the Army Corps of Engineers. Katrina. When those same New Orleanians
were finally permitted to return to the city, they contrived a new medium
of public discourse through which they continued to call those names: the
Katrina refrigerator.

This discourse was entirely contingent upon its scene of enunciation. Prohibited from reentering the city for three weeks or more, with their
length of exile determined by their neighborhood of residence, those New
Orleanians who did make it back and who found their homes still standing
and (in some basic way) habitable confronted an outsized mess. Many of
us have seen the images of mold-covered walls and belongings scattered

Volume 19, Number 2   DOI 10.1215/10407391-2008-001

across dead lawns. Like the graffiti that Susan Stewart describes in *Crimes of Writing*, those sunlit and waterlogged diaries, photographs, and collectibles made for uncomfortable viewing. It was as though New Orleanians had "put their subjectivity in the wrong place" (223). Or rather had it put there for them. These materials constituted an "interruption of the boundaries of public and private space," and they dissolved the "claims of street, façade, exterior, and interior by which the city is articulated" (216).

For locals, one of the most indelible memories of the post-Katrina landscape has to do with the sight of the forlorn and abandoned "iceboxes" lining the area's streets and the specific form of public writing they induced. With the power shut off for weeks, the abandoned city's refrigerators turned into hotboxes rendered useless by what transpired inside of them. As the returnees deposited their wrecked refrigerators curbside for collection, they could not resist the impulse to declaim and once again to name. It was as though the years of taping notes and lists to refrigerator doors, as well as those coy magnetic poetry kits, had primed the city for this moment. The spirit of William Carlos Williams descended. A chapbook of photographs entitled *Spoiled* (2005) documents these refrigerators (Varisco). One—cold white and strapped shut with grey duct tape—has spray painted in large black block letters across its front door: "SMELLS LIKE FEMA." On the side of another model bound with twine: "DICK & DUBYA INC." Prosecuting the case against a more local perpetrator in red paint rather than black: "LEVEE BOARD VICTIM." And most concisely, painted below a magnetic calendar still stuck to a door, the given name (now coupled with a misogynistic epithet) that appeared to name it all and thereby to define this as a singular event: "KATRINA, YOU BITCH."

In the months and years that have followed, the local tenor of the complaint has shifted; so has its vehicle: from the given name to the family name, from the singular to the categorical. This shift first registered in my consciousness during a trip to New Orleans about six months into the "recovery" to visit family members. My nephews—aged four and two at the time—anticipated what would eventually become the characteristic mode of referencing what had come to pass. In the precocious way of children, their language predicted the new semiotic of their community before it had fully emerged. They erected a small city made from blankets, chairs, and toys; then they proceeded to destroy it. They were playing a game they called "storm."

That word would come to dominate the lexicon of post-Katrina New Orleans. As in: "How did your family do in *the storm*?" or "When did

you come back after *the storm?*" or "They didn't reopen after *the storm.*" Although given names still surfaced (as they continue to do) and no official decision was taken to prohibit the phrase "Hurricane Katrina," New Orleanians increasingly communicated with each other in terms that seemed to argue the inadequacy of the name itself—not just this name, Katrina, but any given name. In this new linguistic economy, what had come to pass was generalized. Where given names seek to mark the difference of the individual from the family, "the storm" is categorical. Notwithstanding the definite article, to call what had happened *the storm* is to shift it one step away from the realm of the fully contingent, the historically unique, the absolutely singular. From one familiar perspective, it is in this sense to strip what happened of its eventfulness by making categorical resemblances reappear.

In undertaking this lexical shift, New Orleanians were not, strictly speaking, striking out on their own. In *After the Deluge* (2007), a book that emerged from an installation/exhibition she created for the Metropolitan Museum of Art, the artist Kara Walker writes the following:

> *At this book's inception, the narrative of Hurricane Katrina had shifted precipitously away from the hyperreal horror show presented to the outside world as live coverage of a frightened and helpless populous (relayed by equally frightened and helpless reporters) to a more assimilable legend. Lately, the narrative of the disaster has turned to "security failures," or "the question of race and poverty," or "rebirth." I've heard harrowing anecdotes of survival and humorous tales of rancid refrigerators. And always at the end of these tales, reported on the news, in newspapers, and by word of mouth, always there is a puddle—a murky, unnavigable space that is overcrowded with intangibles: shame, remorse, vanity, morbidity, silence. (7)*

Walker's comments indicate a certain unease with this process of recuperation, the moment when the puddle and its overcrowded residents are stepped over. She describes the spread of euphemistic narratives stripped of euphemism's capacity for consolation. For Walker, as for many who have analyzed the event as a category of experience and analysis, the event is a specific intrusion into the everyday, unsuited for assimilation to the already known. In this sense, the event is a privileged site of the new. It is invested with an uneasy form of hope: the hope that there might be something other than now, accompanied by the fearful knowledge that the shape of the new will exceed what we know. To call what came to pass in New Orleans simply *the storm* would seem to overwrite this unprecedented specificity of the event, as well as the hope and fear it entails.

From Derrida, we learn:

> *An event is always exceptional. This is one possible definition of the event. An event must be exceptional, an exception to the rule. Once there are rules, norms, and hence criteria to evaluate this or that, what happens and what doesn't happen, there is no event. (457)*

To call an event a "storm" is to reduce it to a category already known. It is to take a novel circumstance and strip it of its singularity. William Sewell's recent account of the event as a useful category for the writing of history, which builds upon Marshall Sahlin's event-based arguments in the field of anthropology, suggests that any event worthy of the name produces transformations in the larger social structures that embrace it, such that the old names no longer mean what they once meant. Calling something *the storm* gives the impression of evading this circumstantial novelty.

The process of nominative generalization described here emerges even in specific gestures that seek to contract the frame of naming and to designate the terms of New Orleans's demise. Spike Lee's decision to entitle his HBO documentary *When the Levees Broke* (2006) represents a deliberate response to the naturalizing, "de-eventing" of what had happened to New Orleans. Lee's title and indeed his movie make a specific claim about the precise nature of the Katrina event. Like the movie, Lee's title proposes that it was not Hurricane Katrina itself but rather the nation-state's failure to maintain the city's levees and their subsequent collapse that was to blame for the city's loss. Refusing the perception that what happened in New Orleans was a natural disaster (as Hayden White indicates in his contribution to this issue, there are "no 'tragedies' in nature"), Lee insists that what happened deserves to be thought of as a historical event—a moment involving "surprise, exposure, the unanticipatable" (Derrida 441). Yet, in naming his account *When the Levees Broke*, Lee also signifies upon an old Memphis Minnie blues song, "When the Levee Breaks" (1929), written in part to commemorate the Flood of 1927—one refrain of which opens this introduction. As the Mississippi River's waters rose in the spring of 1927, threatening to breach New Orleans's levees, black New Orleanians were forced by government agencies to shore up those levees. Their labor was not relieved until it was decided to blast open the levees downriver from the city and flood the River Parishes (Kelman 171–96). If Lee assimilates the Hurricane of 2005 to the Flood of 1927, Walker herself ultimately effects a similar recouping of the more recent moment of loss. Despite her palpable distaste for the predictable narrativization of Hurricane Katrina and its redefinition in terms of the already known, Walker suggests the following:

> *The story that has interested me is the story of Muck [. . .]. Black life, urban and rural Southern life, is often related as if it were an entity with a shadowy beginning and a potentially heroic future, but with a soul that is crippled by racist psychosis. One theme in my artwork is the idea that a Black subject in the present tense is a container for specific pathologies from the past and is continually growing and feeding off those maladies. Racist pathology is the Muck, aforementioned. (8, 9)*

Here, Hurricane Katrina effects a Muck that is continuous with rather than a marked break from what has come before. Walker's words and the imagery she chose to include in the installation/exhibition that precipitated her book oscillate: between placing Hurricane Katrina in what Saidiya Hartman, following Fernand Braudel and the *Annales* historians, has called the *longue durée* of racial slavery, and seeking to particularize it as an event in a manner the *Annales* school would have rejected. From the first perspective, Katrina was not only not unpredictable; its place in a centuries-old social structure is all too easy to identify. Walker's Muck recalls "de muck" of Zora Neale Hurston's *Their Eyes Were Watching God* (1937), as well as the hurricane and economic injustice upon which that novel's plot turns. In this context, the appropriate response to Lee's title, *When the Levees Broke*, would seem to be something like: Which time? Which levees? From the second, more event-worthy perspective, the Muck, the storm might be thought of as a substitution for that which is so new we cannot yet name it—a placeholder for something not yet fully present to cognition.

The pressing, silent question here is how one might do justice to the event, where justice is understood to be the taking of an event's full measure. That fundamental question can only be answered, however, once this one has been addressed: how do we know an event has happened? It seems generally clear that an event cannot be announced in advance. Derrida suggests that the event must fall upon us vertically; it must come from a place that never functions as anyone's horizon. But what other qualities signify the present or passing appearance of an event deserving of that signature?

As several of the essays below suggest, it may be precisely the oscillating indecision described above that signals the presence of an event. The idiomatic phrase "I'll know it when I see it" gains a certain analytic force here. The event cannot be known until it is seen. The moment that it is seen, however, it begins to slip away from us: it is "never decided upon." The attention paid here to the event suggests that as it slips away from us, the event draws us across conventional chronological and cartographical divisions of time and space. This capacity for offering a measure different from the clock, the calendar, the empirical map, has long been the attraction of the notion of the event. Here, that capacity is suggested in a collection of essays that "cross-stitch" time and space, to borrow Wai Chee Dimock's useful phrasing. Hayden White identifies flash points when the event has preoccupied Western philosophy and, in particular, theories of history. Dimock indicates how attending to one particular event, Hurricane Katrina, can demonstrate the inadequacy of the national frame for an ethical relationship to history and democracy. Jonathan Elmer shows how the participants in what would appear to be a clear-cut case of historical eventfulness, such as the Haitian revolution, might fail to recognize it (and themselves) as such. Andrew Aisenberg points to a model of social knowledge—Pierre Bourdieu's account of habitus—forged in relationship to the event of the Algerian War and that refuses to abstract the particular conditions of Algerian life. Rebecca Wanzo explains how (white) girls' bodies become events, and how other (brown) girls' bodies are denied event status. Akira Mizuta Lippit traces the exteriorization of the heart onto the other precipitated by the event of the end. In each of these essays, the conventional expectation that "the event" is a phenomenon of punctuality or simultaneity is frustrated. The event in this sense perhaps offers an alternative to the mode of historicism currently dominating the study of culture. In the event, as it were, an alternative to the present might in fact emerge.

LLOYD PRATT is Assistant Professor of English and Core Faculty in African American and African Studies at Michigan State University. He has completed a book manuscript titled "Archives of American Time: Literature and Genre in the Antebellum U.S." His publications include essays in *Novel*, *differences*, and *American Literary History*.

Works Cited   Derrida, Jacques. "A Certain Impossible Possibility of Saying the Event." Trans. Gila Walker. *Critical Inquiry* 33 (Winter 2007): 441–61.

Kelman, Ari. *A River and Its City: The Nature of Landscape in New Orleans*. Berkeley: U of California P, 2006.

McCoy, Minnie [Memphis Minnie], and Joe McCoy. "When the Levee Breaks." Rec. 18 June 1929. *Queen of the Blues: Memphis Minnie*. Columbia, 1997.

Sahlins, Marshall. *Islands of History*. Chicago: U of Chicago P, 1985.

Sewell, William H., Jr. *Logics of History: Social Theory and Social Transformation*. Chicago: U of Chicago P, 2005.

Stewart, Susan. *Crimes of Writing: Problems in the Containment of Representation*. Durham: Duke UP, 1991.

Varisco, Tom. *Spoiled*. New Orleans: Tom Varisco Designs, 2005. www.tomvariscodesigns.com.

Walker, Kara. *After the Deluge*. New York: Rizzoli, 2007.

When the Levees Broke: A Requiem in Four Acts. Dir. Spike Lee. HBO Documentary Films, 2006.

The Historical Event

For the process of truth to begin, something must happen. What there already is—the situation of knowledge as such—generates nothing other than repetition. For a truth to affirm its newness, there must be a *supplement*. This supplement is committed to chance. It is unpredictable, incalculable. It is beyond what is. I call it an event. A truth thus appears, in its newness, because a supplement interrupts repetition.
—Badiou

I never thought we would see the day when an African-American and a woman were competing for the presidency of the United States [. . .]. [T]his is not a piece of history that is happening to someone else; this is happening to us.
—Hillary Clinton

We're on the brink or cusp of doing something important; we can make history. [. . .] We can make history by being, [for] the first time in a very long time, a grass-roots movement of people of all colors.
—Barack Obama

*R*ecent discussion on the periphery of mainstream historical studies has revealed the extent to which "belonging to history" (rather than being "outside of it") or "having a history" (rather than lacking one) have become values attached to certain modern quests for group identity. From the perspective of groups claiming to have been excluded from history, history itself is seen as a possession of dominant groups who claim the authority to decide who or what is to be admitted to history and thereby determine who or what will be considered to be fully human. Even among those groups that pride themselves on belonging to history (here understood as being civilized) or in having a history (here understood as having a real as against a mythical genealogy), it has long been thought that history is written by the victors and to their advantage and that historical writing, consequently, is an ideological weapon with which to double the oppression of already vanquished groups by depriving them of their historical pasts and consequently of their identities as well.

Volume 19, Number 2   DOI 10.1215/10407391-2008-002

Although it has long been claimed that "history" is a place in and a condition of being of everything that is "truly" human and that "history" is a universal process or relationship (like entropy or gravity), "history" itself shows that "history" was invented and cultivated as a learned science in the West, is based on specifically Western, aristocratic, racist, gen(d)eric, and classist preconceptions, and is no more "universalist" in its applicability to other cultures than Christianity or capitalism. So to view "history" as a "gift" of unalloyed value and usefulness to those who are seeking to enter it or belong to it may be delusory. It is within the context of this problematic that I wish to address the question of the nature, meaning, and discursive function of the historical event.

Let me stress that by the term "history," I mean "the past," to be sure, but also something other and much more. Every individual and every group has a past, just by virtue of having a genetic and a cultural endowment of some kind. But a past made up of a genetic and cultural endowment is not the same thing as a historical past. In our time, which is that of late modernity, a specifically historical past is created by professional or in some way socially authorized investigators of what is only a virtual past as long as it has not been established as having really happened on the basis of evidence of a specific kind and authority. This historical past is a construction made by selecting from the wide range of all the events of the human past a specific congeries of those events that can be established as having happened at specific times and places and can be fitted into diachronically organized accounts of a group's self-constitution over time.

As Michael Oakshott has argued, this historical past is quite different from "the practical past" that most of us carry around in our heads in the form of memory, imagination, snippets of information, formulas and practices that we perform by rote, and vague ideas about "history" that we draw on in the course of a day for the performance of tasks as various as running for president of the United States, justifying a policy of war or economic adventure, planning a party, or arguing a case at law (18). The historical past exists only in the books and articles written by professional investigators of pasts and written for the most part for one another rather than for the general public. This historical past is, according to the doxa of the professionals, constructed as an end in itself, has very limited if any practical usefulness, and contributes only minimally to the understanding of what ordinary folk regard as "the present." It is ironic that, as professional historical studies have become more and more scientific, they have become less and less useful for any practical purpose, including the traditional one of educating the laity in the realities of political life. Modern historical studies are genuinely dianoetic in aim and method, contemplative rather than active in kind. For modern historical studies, a historical event is any occurrence that lends itself to investigation by the techniques and procedures currently in force among the guild of professional historians. Such an event may make its appearance in the practical life of a given society or other kind of group, but insofar as it can be studied as a "historical" event, it is moved out of the category of past events that can be utilized for practical purposes and removed into that "historical past" that renders it now only an object of contemplation rather than a tool or instrument to be used in the present for practical ends.

Since the time of Herodotus, there have been conventions, rules, and procedures for deciding what kind of events can be legitimately considered to be "historical," on what grounds and by what kind of evidence events can be established as facts, and how to relate any given historical account of any given body of historical facts to other accounts and facts of a properly historical kind. In modernity, historical events are thought to belong to the class of "natural" events but to be antithetical in kind to "supernatural" events. So, too, historical accounts are thought to belong to the class of narratable processes[1] but to be antithetical to the kind of narratives called "myths" and to any kind of "fiction."

According to the Western ideology of history,[2] "history" came into existence at a particular time and place, developed among the peoples inhabiting that time and place, expanded in time and space with the expansion of Western civilization, and is in fact properly recounted as the story of how this expansion into the rest of the world occurred. "Modern" (itself a Western notion and mode of social existence) practitioners of history purport, of course, to have drained the notion of "the historical" of its cultural specificity as a distinctively Western ideology and to have constituted it as a "soft" but nonetheless universal science. But whereas a modern physical science might be taken up by a given culture without necessarily requiring abandonment of dominant traditional values and institutions, it is questionable whether non-Western cultures can take up "history" without jettisoning much of their traditional cultural baggage—any more than non-Western traditional cultures can take up Christianity or capitalism without losing their distinct identities based on their presumed relationship to a past that may have nothing "historical" about it at all.

Thus, "history," or so it might seem, is or has been for most of the last two millenia a *construction* and a value in the West, while other cultures have chosen to relate to their pasts in ways sometimes similar to but ultimately different from the "historical" way.[3] It is for this, and a number of other reasons, to be sure, that *theories* of history have been developed in recent times, in the West and elsewhere, directed at the identification of ambiguities of the kind usually ascribed to ideologies, myths, and religions rather than those found in scientific disciplines. In other words, there has been an effort in recent times to "deconstruct" history in much the same way that "man," "race," "gender," "literature," "society," and other mainstays of Western humanism have been deconstructed. Excluded and subaltern groups have objected, of course, to this theorization of history as yet another tactic designed to foreclose their claim to "belong to history" quite as much as their oppressors or to "have a history" of their own that founds their identity similarly.

Yet, theory of history (as against historiological theories or theoretical considerations about the nature and uses of historical knowledge) developed within Western culture at a particular moment in the evolution of historical studies, the moment at which it was professionalized, academicized, and began to lay claim to the status of a (modern) science.[4] There can be no science in the modern sense without theory, and indeed it is a sign of the modernity of a given field of scientific activity to be divisible into a "theoretical" and a "practical" (or "applied") dimension. Prior to this moment in its development, historiographical composition was treated as a perfectly "natural" or ordinary activity that could be practiced by anyone endowed with "letters" and the learning required to read old documents or interrogate witnesses of past events effectively. Prior to this moment, differences might be entertained as to the "meaning" that could be derived from the study of past public affairs, especially when claims of a religious or politically sectarian nature regarding certain events of the past were concerned, but these were not so much "theoretical" as, rather, "practical" matters—insofar, especially, as they required the effort to establish "the facts" at issue as a necessary preliminary to the assessment of their possible meaning.

To those for whom the Incarnation or the Resurrection or the Descent of the Holy Spirit were already taken as fact on faith, the problem of the relation of fact to meaning was already resolved relatively easily. By contrast, for the scientific historian, the only possible factuality to be accorded to these allegedly "miraculous" events would be their status as beliefs held by specific people at specific times and places. The factuality of the events themselves would have to be treated as having been based on evidence of a kind not to be admitted in historical (or, more precisely, historiological) discourse.

Obviously, in cases like the last mentioned, scientific historians would be concerned as much about the nature of the events under question as they would about the nature of the evidence offered in support of their factuality. In history, any reported event of whatever kind, natural or miraculous as the case might be, has to be treated as a potential fact since to rule out any given reported event as impossible in advance of investigation of the evidence of its occurrence would violate the empiricist principles governing historical inquiry from the origins of the genre. But the very distinction between natural events and miraculous events indicates the importance of the distinction between event and fact in historiological discourse. Since a miraculous event is a manifestation of a power outside of nature and a fortiori outside of history, a miraculous event is the one kind of event that can never be treated as a historical fact.

The canonical version of the distinction between an event and a fact has it that "a fact is an event under a description"—where "description" can be understood as consisting of a perspicuous listing of attributes of the event—or a "predication"—by which an event is assigned to its proper kind and, usually, given a proper name.[5] An event cannot enter into a history until it has been established as fact. From which it can be concluded: events happen, facts are established. A fact may be construed as a happening in speech or writing and in this sense conceived as an event. But facts are events of a special kind: they are events in speech that are about other speech events and other kinds of events beyond or outside of speech. On this account, a historical fact would differ from other kinds of fact by virtue of the rules prevailing in historical discourses for determining when a given event could be described as the kind of event properly characterized as "historical."

Now, in general, people who know something about the issue have little difficulty defining "historical event" and distinguishing historical from other kinds of events, pseudo events, and nonevents, natural, supernatural, imaginary, illusory, and so on. And historians in general have good or at least tried and trusted rules for determining how events are to be established as facts or established as having really happened rather than only appearing to have happened or as having been falsely reported as having happened. None of these procedures is scientific in the sense of requiring experimental replication of the event under laboratory conditions or the subsumption of a given event to the causal laws or relationships governing the class of events to which it may belong. But they are good enough for the kind of crude social uses to which historical knowledge has been contrived to contribute since its invention in Greece during the fifth century B.C.E.

So, let us grant that there are events and there are facts. Let us grant, too, that there are series of events and structures of events that can be factualized, which is to say, dated, placed, described, classified, and named well enough to permit a distinction between "atomic" or individual facts and something like "molar" or macro-facts—"large" facts such as "The Russian Revolution of 1917" or "big" facts such as "The Renaissance." This would allow us to imagine a wide range of "historical facts" that would make up that "history" that is the object of study of "historians."

But this way of thinking about history—as an aggregation of facts—begs the question of the status of those "events" that are the content, referent, or necessary condition of facts.

There has been a great deal of discussion of late about the event in general and about the historical event specifically. In historiography, the evental status of the Holocaust is a matter of extensive debate: is or was the Holocaust an event unique to history and therefore incomparable to (or incommensurable with) other events of a similar kind? So, too, for the event now called 9/11. Was the attack on the Twin Towers on September 11, 2001, an utterly new kind of event, indeed emblematic of a new epoch and paradigmatic therefore of a category of historical events hitherto unimaginable and requiring, consequently, a search for new principles of explanation for its contextualization? Or was it simply an event that happened to have been unexpected in the United States, an event only unimaginable in that context—since, obviously, it was all too imaginable among its perpetrators?

In most of these discussions, that an event occurred does not have to be established. What is at question is the nature of the event, its relative novelty, the scope and intensity of its impact, and its meaning or what it reveals about the society in which it took place. "Things will never be the same," it has been said of both of the two events; "It is the end of American innocence," it is said of 9/11; "Never again," has been one response to the Holocaust.

While responses such as these are both understandable and, if understood figuratively, more than adequately justified, it is not always registered how such responses implicitly presume a precise idea of what a historical event—as against a natural event—consists of. A natural event, such as an earthquake or an avalanche, will always have been conceivable, imaginable, possible, and, in some locales, even probable. The disastrous consequences of such events attach to the human beings who insufficiently prepared for the occurrence of this type of event in the physical areas affected by them. Thus, although the effects of such events on human beings and groups in a particular place can appropriately be described as "disastrous," even "tragic," the same epithets could be used to describe the events themselves in only a figurative way. There are no "disasters" and certainly no "tragedies" in nature. The fact that there are plenty of events in history to which such epithets can be legitimately or at least appropriately applied tells us something about the extent to which "history," in spite of its efforts to become scientific, remains indentured to mythical notions of the cosmos, the kinds of events that occur in it, and the kinds of knowledge we can have of them.

In our time, many other events made possible by new technologies and modes of production and reproduction have changed the nature of institutions and practices that had remained virtually unchanged for millennia (for example, warfare and health care) and changed them so radically that it has become impossible to write a history of, say, war as a tale of continuous development from the Stone Age to only yesterday. Weapons of mass destruction cause a quantum leap in the *history* of warfare. Antibiotics and genetic engineering change definitively the nature of health care for the foreseeable future. All this suggests that the principles that make historical change possible in the first place may themselves undergo change. Or to put it another way: change itself changes, at least in history if not in nature. If it does, then so, too, can the nature of events change as well.[6]

Can we imagine a new *kind* of event breaking in on our world that might manifest evidence of another, alternative system of existence that differs utterly from our own? Fantasies of alien cultures in outer space and theories of parallel or antithetical universes reflect the wish, hope, or fear of the existence of such alternative places from which new and strange events might emanate. Such fantasies may seem delusory, but they are no more so than our notion of "history" considered as a process made up of conflicting and mutually exclusive societies, cultures, and races each vying with the other for *Lebensraum* and the resources to allow one or another to prevail over all contenders.

But not only that: history itself, with its division into past and present that parses human nature into earlier and later avatars whose differences are often thought to be more striking than any similarities between them, already contains more than enough evidence of radical discontinuity over time. Indeed, history is thought to be composed of events of a kind that effect changes in the common human substrate that amount more to mutations than simply variations on the common heritage. Imagine how different is the kind of event that modernist technology is capable of producing from those that might have been familiar to a peasant of the twelfth century. Certain events in modernity—space travel, genetic engineering, atomic weaponry—are so utterly different from anything previously thought possible that even a modern peasant or bourgeois might be forgiven for taking them as "miracles." So different, indeed, are certain events of the present moment from anything preceding them that we can readily understand why certain intellectuals might be impelled to speak of "the end of history" or, like Marx, to speak of everything that has happened up until now as "prehistory" or a prelude to the real drama of a humankind that has finally come into its own and escaped what we had thought of as history *and* nature before.

To be sure, Western historical studies have just recently recovered from a sustained attack, mounted from within its own ranks, on the very notion of "event." I will not recapitulate details of the attack by the *Annales* school in the decades following World War II upon the fetishistic nature of the historical event and the mythical nature of the idea that historical processes possess the kind of coherence found in stories, fables, and legends. Modern(ist) philosophers of history typically distinguish between a tradition of conventional, popular, or amateur historiography centered on events and concerned to dramatize them, on the one side, and a more scientific and enlightened historiography centered on structures, long-term processes (*la longue durée*), and "slow" time, on the other. "Event-history," it was held, was little more than entertainment and little less than fantasy insofar as it fed the dreams and illusions of a bankrupt humanism. In fact, the French historian Fernand Braudel tried to diminish the focus on the event in historical research because he saw it as the mainstay of a narrativist approach to history, which made history into a drama and substituted emotional gratification for the intellectual satisfaction of science in the process (see Ricoeur).

As a matter of fact, the historiological notion of event is much closer to the dramatic or rather the dramatistic than it is to any possible scientific conception thereof. Historical narratives run much too smoothly to support any claim to realistic representation of the events they feature as their subject matter. Unlike the kind of natural events (or sets of events) studied by the physical sciences, real historical events run rather roughly and raggedly, largely as a result of the intervention of human agents and agencies into the courses they were originally meant to follow.

Here we encounter another topos in the modernist discourse on the event, that which distinguishes between natural events and historical events on the basis of the presence of human beings—their motivations, their intentions, their desires, their drives—in their enactment. Drama, like epic, is a *mode* of oral, imagistic, gestural, or literary presentation that sets forth an action as a *series* of events within a finite scene but differs from epic in the assignment of different degrees of significance to events in such a way as to permit the series to be grasped as a *sequence* with a beginning, middle, and end. A historical sequence is periodized or parsed into acts and scenes, each of which is related to what follows as a realization or fulfillment of what had come before. But this raises the question: what is the difference between an event that terminates and one that begins a sequence? Or: is a historical event a sign of a rupture in a series and a point of *metamorphosis* from one level, phase, or aspect of the historical continuum to another? Or is it a sign of *transition* from one phase of a continuum to another?

So much is suggested by Alain Badiou's metaphysical discussion of event in *Being and Event*, a discussion neatly summarized in *Infinite Thought*.[7] He assumes that being is everything that is the case and that there is nothing that is not the case. Nothing new can ever be added to being and therefore no event—understood as an eruption of something coming from outside the totality of being—could ever take place. And yet events *seem* to take place all the time, at least to observers or chroniclers of happenings in the real world. This "seeming to take place" could be construed as an event, but it would belong to consciousness rather than to the world exterior to it.

So how is this kind of event possible? As I understand it, Badiou thinks that events *seem* to occur because there is a disparity between being, on the one side, and the knowledge of being, on the other. Event occurs when knowledge of some hitherto unknown aspect of being has to be added to what had been previously known about being. It is, as it were, this "shock" to the knowledge-system by the insistent nature of a newly discovered truth about being that registers as an event to consciousness. In reality, Badiou argues, a new bit of knowledge is only apparently new: it is like the discovery of a hitherto unknown prime number in mathematics. It was always "there" (which is to say, was always "nowhere" but among the universe of numbers) only awaiting (as it were) that computer which is endlessly generating new prime numbers of all but infinite length for its registration. As thus envisaged, event is like the sudden awareness that what had been thought of as the last prime number was only the next to the last and, in fact, is, as the computer continues to spit out new prime numbers, rapidly shrinking in rank and substance with each new prime, the penultimate prime number moves down or back as the newest prime appears.

Now, all this would seem to have little to do with any possible understanding of events that occur in ordinary daily experience (whatever that is) or as envisaged by conventional wisdom or by such "practical" disciplines as those cultivated in the human and social sciences. And this is because it is already generally presumed that event merely indicates an occurrence *unanticipated* by current knowledge about the world and its processes.

For example, the important question about events occurring in what Paul Veyne calls "the sublunary world" of "history" is whether any given event is assimilable to one or another of the received knowledge systems available to a given community or whether the event in question requires the revision or even the total abandonment of the system previously thought capable of adequately identifying, classifying, and determining any event's "propriety" (157). If there is any metaphysical dimension to this notion of event, it attaches to the status of "history" understood as a sphere of existence inhabited by human beings and subject to laws or principles that belong to but deviate slightly from those that govern the rest of "nature." To be sure, knowledge of this "history" does not include all of the human beings that have ever lived or will have lived over the course of worldly time. Knowledge of history is always fragmentary, incomplete, and partial, which is one reason that events of a specifically "historical" kind can occur and will continue to occur and indeed cannot not occur for the "foreseeable" future. But the historical event begins to look suspiciously like the kind of event that Badiou characterized as a "supplement" to being-in-general. It depends on the positing of a knowledge of being and therefore a knower of it as a condition of possibility of its occurrence. Which means that specifically historical events could not occur before a specifically historical kind of knowledge existed. It would have no ground or context against which to display its newness.

On the other hand, a historical event will appear as new only insofar as it can be recognized as inherently or substantively or potentially belonging to the class of events already recognized as "historical" but is apprehended, at the same time, as being exotic to that class. As thus envisaged, any "new" historical event seems to be both in and out of "the historical." Here is where "historical research" enters: its aim is to establish whether the new event belongs to "history" or not, or whether it is some other kind of event. The event in question need not be new in the sense of having only recently arrived to historical consciousness. For the event may have already been registered as having happened in legend, folklore, or myth, and it is, therefore, a matter of identifying its historicity, narrativizing it, and showing its propriety to the structure or configuration of the context in which it appeared. An example and even a paradigm of this situation would be the well-known "search for the historical Jesus" or the establishment of the historicity (or ahistoricity) of the "Jesus" who was represented in the Gospels, not only as a worker of miracles but as Himself the supreme miracle of miracles, the Messiah or God Incarnate whose death and resurrection can redeem the world.

The idea that historical events could not have occurred before the idea of history and the category of the historical had been invented is only a logical paradox. Any right-thinking person would know that the idea of history and the category of the historical must have arisen from somebody's reflection on the kind of events that manifestly differed from some other kind of event, so that the term "history" and the category of "the historical" must derive their meaning from their references to this special kind of event. But let us try to imagine a time before which the idea of history and the category of the historical existed, a time when a number of different kinds of events had been identified but not events of the historical kind. On the evidence available, it seems that the Greeks, who are supposed to have invented the idea of history as an inquiry into the past and the genre of history writing as an account of past events established by such inquiry as having happened, apparently had no word with the signified of our word for "history."

Thus, Greek ἡ ἱστορία *(historia)* will start by meaning only "inquiry" and then, by metonymy of result for the activity that produces it, come to mean the "findings" resulting from the inquiry and, beyond that, by synecdoche, become a name—"the history"—for the events described in the account understood as "what happened in the (or a) past"—or something like that. The Greek word for happenings in the past was τὰ γεγενημένα (*ta gegenēmena*), but the term most used to name an *account* of past happenings (whether based on "inquiry" or received tradition) was *logos* (ὁ λόγος). Whence Thucydides' dismissal of Herodotus as a (mere) "logographer" or teller of stories about the past in order to distinguish what he himself was doing in his "inquiries" into the past and analyses of its processes.

And it should be noted that "logographer" was the term used to characterize an inquirer into the *recent* past in contrast to what might be called (according to Antonin Liakos) an "archaio-lographer," who investigated the *remote* past.[8] Thucydides investigated the recent rather than the remote past in order to identify the causes of the wars between Athens and Sparta, so he would qualify as a logographer as much as Herodotus. But his inquiry was not more systematic than that of Herodotus, only differently so—inasmuch as he seems to have used principles of Hippocratean medicine to serve as a model for how to read the symptoms of the plague that destroyed or fatally weakened the Greek city-states and their empires, while Herodotus was content with the kind of general principles enunciated in pre-Socratic philosophy for his explanations of the events he recounted (explanations of the "what goes up must come down" variety). It was the *kind* of systematicity he used that earned for Thucydides the (modern) title of the first "scientific" historian. Which might be taken to mean that he not only placed events in stories but also provided an argument for their relevance to his aim of explaining the causes and effects of the events he was investigating.

On this account, Herodotus can be credited with having invented the specifically historical event and suggesting its difference from the kinds of events that derived from the actions of gods and spirits. Thucydides can then be credited with having invented a version of historical method or procedures for studying and analyzing, rather than merely reporting, what happened in the past in order to understand the present. But whether he was actually "doing" history or bringing a new method to the analysis of the kinds of events Herododus had investigated is a moot point, it being undecidable whether specifically "historical" events are subsumable under general laws or not. In any case, it was left to the Romans to provide the word *historia*—with its primary meaning of tale or story understood as the kind of account "proper" to the rendition of a series of events into a "history"—as a basis for the notion of the historical event as the kind of event that, although occurring in real rather than imaginary life, could be legitimately presented in the form(s) of the kinds of tales and fables previously told of gods, demons, ghosts, heroes, and other such supernatural beings. With this development, I would suggest, the idea of history as a truthful account of events that really happened in the past cast in the form of story with a plot is achieved. And this provides at least one way of identifying a specifically historical event. As Paul Ricoeur puts it: a historical event is a real event capable of serving as an element of a "plot." Or, as Louis O. Mink used to say: a historical event is one that can truthfully be described in such a way as to serve as an element of a narrative (Ricoeur 208).

All this implies that events are not made "historical" solely by virtue of having really happened, having happened in a specific time in the past and at a specific place in this world, and having had some identifiable effect on the contexts into which they erupted. And this because a list of such events, even a list of events in chronological order, might constitute an annals or a chronicle but hardly a history. In order for a given singular event, set, or series of events to qualify as "historical," the event, set, or series must also be validly describable as if they had the attributes of elements in a *plot* of a story.[9]

Now, the mention of the word *plot* raises another specter that, for professional historians, is almost as threatening as the word *myth*. Not only because the word *plot* is the English translation of the Greek *mythos* but also because *plot* is typically thought to be the device that gives to literary fictions their explanatory effect.[10] The debate over how the insertion of an event into a series in such a way as to transform it into a sequence and provide thereby some equivalent of an explanation for its occurrence—this is a long debate and too long even to summarize here. Suffice it to say that, for our purposes, plot or what I have chosen to call *emplotment* is common to all the kinds of narrative discourse: mythical, fictional, or historical. Thus, it is possible to say that if myths, fictional stories, and histories share a common form (the story, fable, tale, parable, allegory, whatever), they also share a common content, which, following Frank Ankersmit, we may call "narrative substance."[11] The concept of "narrative substance" allows us to say that the historical event, unlike the natural event, is narratable.[12]

The *doxa* of modern professional historical research has it that there are no plots *in* history (the events of the past) any more than there could be a large, all-encompassing, overall plot *of* History (in the sense of a plan or predetermined end, aim, purpose, or telos of the whole trajectory of human development, from the obscure origins to the unimaginable end).

The objection to the so-called master narratives of history, the rejection of which, according to Lyotard, is supposed to be the dominant characteristic of postmodernist thought, is that such fantastic notions as "providence," "fate," "destiny," "progress," "the dialectic," and so on are nothing but residues of mythical and religious dreams of the kind long left behind by "modernity." The general objection to the "master narratives" is that they represent a kind of *teleological* thinking that has had to be overcome for the modern sciences of nature to take shape. There is no teleology in nature, and inasmuch as history belongs to nature (rather than the reverse)—or so it is thought—there can be no teleology in history. And this includes local as well as universal history.

To be sure, human beings and human groups typically *think* teleologically, which is to say, make plans for current and future activities in the light of envisioned ends, aims, purposes. One could speak of human intentions as end oriented and, indeed, in a way that permitted one to use *intentionality* as a basis for distinguishing human from animal nature. But as the poet says, "The best laid plans of mice and men . . . ," and the *doxa* tells us, "The road to perdition is paved with good intentions." Human beings and institutions may very well plan their activities and practices with an end in view, but to suggest that the destinies of individuals and groups can be predetermined in the way the destiny of an oak tree is pre-determined by the acorn from which it springs is a possibility at once comforting and horrifying. Comforting because it takes responsibility away from the subject-agent of history, horrifying because it takes responsibility away from the subject-patient of history. Besides, as it is said, determinism is always what governs other people, never one's own self—except when one wishes to avoid responsibility for a specific action.

But what if it is possible that human beings are both free and determined, responsible and not responsible, at one and the same time for their actions? To think in this way is, of course, a scandal for the philosopher and foolishness for the man of common sense. And yet . . . .

Near the origin of Western philosophy and specifically in the legendary teachings of the founder of Stoicism, Zeno of Citium (d. 265 B.C.E.), we encounter the association of the notion of "event" with that of "destiny" that was to become a commonplace of thought about time on down to Heidegger, Ricoeur, and Badiou. Zeno seems to have taught that every incident occurring in the life of a person was interpretable as evidence of providence's working to turn what would otherwise be a meaningless jumble of events into a destiny (with its sense that the end of a life occurs not only at a particular time but also at a particular place—whence our notion of a *destin*ation as the place we are headed toward).

Here, to be sure, the terms *event* and *destiny* are translated into the elements of a drama with a presumed beginning, middle, and end, a denouement, and a falling off of action after the scene of recognition (*anagnorisis*); and they function more as schemata than as concepts, elements of myth rather than of science, and exude the odor of narrative rather than that of argument. Of course, etymology explains nothing, but the mythological relation between event and destiny indicates the ways in which, in poetic thinking, a problematical term like *event*, with its connotation of both meaningfulness and meaninglessness, can function as an operator in a process in which an image of formal coherency (destiny, fate, *moira*, *telos*) can be used to endow chaos with cosmos. In any event, the relating of event to destiny as figure to fulfillment gave me some insight into what was, to me, a lexicographical surprise: my *Roget's* treatment of "destiny" as an *antonym* of "event" (166).[13]

I was looking for the antonym of "event" because I wanted to begin my thought about the historical event by placing it within the matrix of Aristotle's hermeneutic square, in order to discern what might be its contradictories, contraries, and implicants (ch. 7, no. 19). If "event" is treated as a concept, then precisely because it is a concept, it must have an opposed or antithetical term that tells us what would be its contradictory. The convention that sets "event" in a relationship of contradictoriness to "destiny" suggests that, perhaps, an event can at least be known to be related to the field on or against which it happens, as a "part" of a process *can be opposed* to the "whole" of which it is a part. The event can never be the whole of the process of which it is a part, because "destiny" names the whole process of which any given event is only a part.

But then that leaves us with the problem of identifying the contrary of *event*'s antithetical term, that is, *destiny*, which must be, according to Aristotle's way of reasoning, the "non-destinal," or anything that is not headed anywhere, has no proper place, no substance, and is therefore only a pseudo event, element of a pseudo destiny (Rämö). And this suggests that whatever an event will finally turn out to be, the one thing that we can say about it is that it is not destiny, that it is not the whole process that might ultimately endow contingency with meaning, the meaning of *place* in a sequence, placefulness, or situation. This is to say that the event is not and can never be the whole of whatever it is a part, element, or factor—except at the end, when it comes into its own or finds a place it was destined to come to at last. Maybe this is what Heidegger had in mind when he spoke of history as *Dasein*'s "on-the-way-ness" to a place it would never reach and *Dasein*'s fate as *eine Verwendung*, a meandering, a wending, a drift, slide, or roaming that always ends short of a destination, because destiny implies propriety and mankind is *ohne Eigenschaften*.[14]

But now, in order to fill out our form of reasoning, we must posit the *contrary* (not the contradictory) of event itself, and if, as we have already indicated, it cannot be either the whole (which is destiny) or those other parts of the whole besides itself, then the event must be something else, which is neither part nor whole of the whole, which can only be, I think, some combination of the non-evental and non-destinal. Whence, I presume, the modern(ist) juxtaposition of event and structure as a model for a scientific construal of the nature of the historical. In modernist thinking, structure stands in for destiny, providence, fate, fortune, and the like, insofar as—as in the structuralist paradigm—the "meaning" of things human must turn out to be nothing other than their form, raised up against a "nature" that, more and more, reveals its meaning as little more than "chaos." In this model, the event is what disturbs structure, whatever it is that resists incorporation into what is at any given moment "the case." From an ontological point of view, every event is an embarrassment and a challenge, an embarrassment to the comprehensiveness of structure and a challenge to structure's power to provide meaning to everything that is the case. Small wonder that structuralism has turned out to be the very antithesis of a historical worldview. As a plenum of events each one of which is an individual happening (a kind of "concrete universal" resistant to subsumption to any universal, on the one hand, and to reduction to an aggregate of particularities, on the other), history appears to be little more than the condition from which any structuralist would wish to escape.

Now, all of this could be quite bewildering if it were not for the fact that, outside the various fields of historical studies and in those disciplines where something like a "historical method" remains a prin- ciple component in their operations, the notion of the event has been pretty much discredited as an element of scientific thought. The notion of event remains a staple of a certain kind of literary writing, of the novel, of the romance, of poetry, of theology, and of myth, and so on—kinds of composition called "imaginative" or "imaginary" and generally related by genealogical affiliation to prescientific ways of thinking, explaining, and living with the world rather than living off of it. And indeed, there is a whole body of contemporary writing that suggests that the notion of event and especially the notion of event informing and authorizing a belief in the reality of "history" is a displacement from mythical modes of thinking and actually has more in common with a religious idea of miracle than with any scientific conception of what an event could possibly be.

This body of contemporary writing has its origins in the hybrid genre of the "historical novel" that, contrary to the rules of the game just being formulated by the historical profession, faces openly the problem of the relation between the past and the present, the ambiguity of "the recent past" and the paradox of the presence of the past in the present—as in Scott, Manzoni, and Dumas, but also Balzac, Stendhal, Flaubert, Dickens, Tolstoy, Thackeray, Trollope, Conrad, and a host of lesser lights. It is the historical novel that lays the groundwork of the modernist novel, in which the event begins to dissipate and the line between the past and the present becomes as scumbled as that between consciousness and the unconscious. Modernism, for all its trumpeting of the novelty of "the way we live now," restores the dignity of the archaic, formerly abandoned by history because of its lack of documentation and consigned to the tender mercies of archeology and the "antiquities," as a source of meaning for "reality."

As Auerbach and others argue, modernism is anything but a flight from realism and history. It liberates the historical event from the domesticating suasions of "plot" by doing away with "plot" itself. Moreover, far from abandoning reality for fantasy, modernism shows how much of the fantastic is contained in "the real." Modernism not only extends the reach of the historical event horizontally, allowing it to wash into adjacent areas of time, it reveals the depths of the historical event, showing how many layers of meaning it conceals, how labile are its pulsions, how resistant to concretion it is.

Modernism probes the depths of the historical event in much the same way that psychoanalysis probes the depths of the psychic event.[15] And indeed, it changes the relation between the event and its context by dissolving the line between them. All of which adds up to the creation of a new mode of literary writing in which the line between factual discourse and fictional discourse is blurred in a kind of writing (the infamous *écriture*) that would destroy the artistic authority of the earlier, nineteenth-century realism. Henceforth, history, the historical event, and historicality itself are taken over by a new kind of writing that, for want of a better term, we may call postmodernist.

However, it is not enough to summon up a "new kind of writing" to account for changes in the way that "history" and its typical content "event" are construed in our time. For a distinctively "historical" way of accounting for the invention of a "new kind of writing" requires us to identify the new "content" or phenomenon for the representation of which the new kind of writing is thought to be adequate. I have already alluded to the "modernist event" as such a content, phenomenon, or referent. Now, I will go further and suggest that the "substance" of the "content" of this new kind of event is provided in the historiotheticized idea of "trauma." The modern provenance of the term *traumatic* is medicine where it is used to characterize a wound, more precisely a penetration of the skin and bone, and the resultant scar, physical and psychical, caused by the penetration. When used to characterize a certain kind of historical event, the term *trauma* and its adjectival form *traumatic* are quite conventional and mean something like a massive blow to a social or political system that requires the kind of adjustment, adaptation, or reaction that any organism must make if it is to survive it.

In the theory of psychoanalysis, however, the terms *trauma* and *traumatic* are used (metaphorically, at first) to indicate a shock to the organism that has the somatic and/or psychical effect of "unbinding" the "drives" formerly held in some kind of equilibrium and thereby producing neurotic or psychopathic states (paranoia, hysteria, obsessiveness, etc.) resulting in the dysfunctionality of the organism. This physicalist conception of trauma (developed by Breuer and Freud in the 1890s) does not differ in any special way from its historiological counterpart in which the historical event is viewed as a significant disturbance of a historical (social) system that throws its institutions, practices, and beliefs into disarray and results in group behaviors similar to those manifested in the conditions of hysteria, paranoia, fetishism, and so on.

But Freud and other psychoanalysts later developed another idea of trauma that presupposed a distinctly "historical" element inasmuch as it involved an element of "afterwardness" (*Nachträglichkeit*) understood as a "(temporally) deferred effect" on the organism strikingly similar to what historiology took to be a specifically *historical* relation between the past and the present. For now, Freud characterized the psychic dimension of trauma as not only a (sudden and disruptive) shock to the organism but one that left *in the psyche of certain kinds of individuals* a kind of place devoid of meaning until, under the press of a later event similar in aspect to the original experience of incursion, this place was suddenly enlivened or animated so as to disclose a meaning so overdetermined as to wound the organism once more—in fact, to render it doubly wounded, first, by the recall of the original scene of incursion and the sudden discovery of its meaning, and then, by a repetition once more of the original move of fending it off from consciousness, now attended, as it were, by feelings of guilt for not having recognized what it had been in the first place.

There is a similarity between the way historians conceive the relationship between the historical past and the present, on the one side, and Freud's conception of the relationship between a traumatic event in the life of an individual and its "return" to consciousness at some later time but with an impact strong enough to render the individual dysfunctional. The idea of the traumatizing event permits Freud to postulate a "secret history" of an individual and, by extension, of a whole people or nation, against which the "official" account of its past is to be comprehended as an alibi or sublimation in response to guilt feelings derived from the original act. In *Moses and Monotheism* (*Der Mann Moses und die Monotheistische Religion*), the theory of the traumatizing historical event permits Freud to postulate a terrible crime in the Hebrew past, that is, the murder of Moses by the people he had saddled with an impossible obligation to the Law, which accounts for the perfervid asceticism, self-discipline, failure to become a nation, and restless wandering, guilt, and melancholy of the Jewish people. It is "the return of the repressed memory" of this primal crime—the murder of the Father—that constitutes the past-in-the-present that the Jews, at least, live as "history."[16]

To be sure, Freud's notion of the "history" of the Hebrew people bears all the marks of myth—in spite of the gestures it makes to current historical scholarship and his own efforts to sound "scientific." But the idiom of mythagogy is utterly appropriate for the kind of cause-effect relationship between past and present that he calls *nachträglich* (belated). It is "magical," involving as it does such notions as action at a distance, deferred effect, latency, and the like. Freud does not reject or question the conventional historical idea that an event at a given time and place "spreads out," as it were, in both time and space, producing other events to be treated as "effects" of a prior "cause." But he does postulate another kind of event, the true nature and effects of which get buried in individual and collective memory, lie latent therein for an indeterminate amount of time, and then, in response to some later event of similarly invasive effect, resurfaces in a *form* that at once reveals and conceals its remote prototype. Such an event, the traumatic event, has the structure of the figure-fulfillment model of Hebrew *and* Christian theodicy.

In the figure-fulfillment model, a *significant* historical event will be recognized by its double occurrence, the first time as an *intimation* of a possibility of meaning and the second time as an "expletion," a filling out or a fulfillment of what was only implicit or, to use a psychological term, latent in the earlier event. The theological models are well known: the substitution of the ram for Isaac in Abraham's intended sacrifice of his son is an anticipation of the Law of Moses that "fulfills" it; the Fall of Adam that is fulfilled in the Resurrection of Christ, and so on. A secularized equivalent of the figure-fulfillment model in historiological theory would be something like the argument that the remote but determinant cause of the French Revolution was the Protestant Reformation. In Tocqueville's argument, the Reformation already contains in embryo, as it were, the Revolution that brings down the Old Regime. Mind you, it is not that the earlier event predetermines the later event, or that the later event is to be considered the *telos* toward which everything tends once the Reformation has occurred. This is not a teleological idea of historical causation. No one could have predicted the outbreak of the French Revolution on the basis of whatever knowledge they might have had about the Reformation. It is only after the Revolution had occurred that it became possible to see what the Reformation had made possible.

So it is with Freud's so-called "traumatic" or "traumatizing" event. There is no absolute necessity for an early molestation of a child by an adult to surface in later life as "trauma" and produce debilitating effects in the adolescent or adult. It all depends upon the occurrence of a second event similar to the earlier one but openly identifiable as what it is or intended to be that triggers the recognition-repression response that now buries or otherwise blocks access to both events and relegates them to a space outside of the "real history" to which they belong. The equivalent in real history would be a kind of schizo-historiology in which the desire to know or obsession with the past is attended by an equally strong aversion to or rejection of any knowledge of the past that threatens the benign version of historical reality constructed as a screen against the threatening truth. I do not have space to go into the matter now, but I would suggest that Kantorowicz's theory of "the king's two bodies" analyzes a topos of such schizo-history.

It should be stressed, of course, that Freud was neither a professional historian nor a professional philosopher (of history) and that neither professional historians nor professional philosophers had any particular reason to regard his concept of the traumatic event as a contribution to the scientific study of history, the historical past, or the historical relation between the past and the present. On the contrary, it may well be that Freud borrowed contemporary myths or notions about history as a model for how to conceptualize a relation between the past and the present of a given individual or nation or people or indeed any group whatsoever in order to conceptualize the kind of relation between present and past he wished to call "traumatic." Freud was an amateur or dilettante in history, archeology, and anthropology, and he was interested in any kind of knowledge that could be turned to therapeutic use in the treatment of psychologically induced maladies. In other words, he was interested in "the practical past" rather than in the historical past composed by and distilled into the learned tomes of professional historians, anthropologists, and archeologists for the enlightenment of their professional peers.[17]

So although he used the work of professional scholars in other fields of inquiry, he was less interested in contributing to those fields of study than using whatever of their lore that could be helpful in conceptualizing a possible treatment for individuals (and groups) suffering from the malady known at that time as "melancholy," a depressive condition that became chronic when an individual sustained an unthinkable loss of a loved object that the normal or conventional modes of "mourning" failed to alleviate.

Now, the important theoretical point about Freud's psychoanalytical concept of trauma consists in the fact that, according to Freud himself, there is no such thing as an inherently traumatic *event*. Even the most horrendous kind of loss is responded to by different individuals in different ways, some in the mode of traumatization, others in the mode of mourning, still others in the various modes of sublimation, repression, or symbolization that take place in the process of "working through" the experience of loss. And here it is necessary to stress again the differences between a medical or physiological notion of trauma and the psychological, psychosomatic, or psychoanalytical idea of it. From a physicalist point of view, there could be inherently traumatic events, which would be any event of sufficiently violent force to threaten the destruction of the organism, individual or collective. That such a notion of historical event already exists in the repertory of professional historians is indicated by their use of the concept of "crisis" as a condition through which groups as well as individuals can suffer. But from the standpoint of the psychoanalytical notion of trauma, there are crises and there are crises. Not all crises, especially the physical ones endured by the organism, are traumatizing of the groups or individuals affected by them. Indeed, trauma names only a particular kind of response to crisis, the way in which it is (only) apperceived rather than perceived as the thievery of self that it will later, under the press of a similar event, be both perceived and understood to have been. What could be a more "historical," "historiological," or "historiographical" way of construing the specifically "historical event"? Or to put it another way: what could be a more historiological way of construing a certain kind of psychosomatic event (whether the soma in question be that of an individual or that of a group)?

Is it possible that the specifically historical event is a happening that occurs in some present (or in the experience of a living group), the nature of which cannot be discerned and a name given to it because it manifests itself only as an "eruption" of a force or energy that disrupts the ongoing system and forces a change (the direction or trajectory of which is unknowable until it is launched or entered upon), the end, aim, or purpose of which can only be discerned, grasped, or responded to at a later time? But not just any old "later time." Rather, that later time when the eruption of what seems to be in some way affiliated with an earlier event reveals or seems to reveal in the fact of that affiliation the "meaning," significance, gist, even foretelling, though in a masked and obscure way, both of the original event and the later one. Such that the later event can be plausibly represented in a narrative in which it is the fulfillment (or derealization) of the meaning having lain latent and now made manifest retrospectively in the earlier one.

If that turned out to be the case, it would be . . . a miracle.

HAYDEN WHITE is University Professor, Emeritus, at the University of California and Professor of Comparative Literature at Stanford University.

Notes   1   Or dramatic processes, by which I mean processes that feature conflict between human beings and other real or imagined forces, powers, and the like, the end or resolution of which turns out to be illuminable of the action leading up to it but in no way foreseeable from any given moment in the process as a whole. The plot types of the principal genres of Western drama serve as models of counterparts in real history, not in any fictionalizing way but because the kinds of conflicts they schematize are latently possible in the kinds of societies that, as in the West, are capable of having "a history."

2   By "ideology of history," I mean the view that history is not only a science of the relation between the past and the present but that it is uniquely adequate to the disclosure of the ways that humanity creates itself over time.

3   The same can be said of two other ways of representing historical processes in the West, the annals form and the chronicle form. Such genres may feature genuinely historiological motifs but do not add up to or fulfill the contract implicit in composition of a history. See White, "Value." On different ways of representing the "historical past," see the arguments advanced by Goody in *The Theft of History*, the title of which refers, Goody tells us, "to the take-over of history by the west" (1); Hacking; and Sahlins.

4   I am trying to introduce some Heideggerian language into the discussions about history, historical knowledge, historical consciousness, and the like: thus, I use the term *history* in the many senses it has in Heidegger's *Being and Time* (see ch. 5, sect. 72–77) and then use *historial* to mean "history-like," *historiology* to mean the real, para-, pseudo, or pretended "science of history," *historiosophy* to mean "the kind of wisdom one is supposed to derive from the study of history," *historiography* to mean "the writing about history," and so on, possibly, even to *historiogony*, *historionomy*, etc. It is a useless gesture, and I have no hope that it will be taken up in Anglophone discourse, first, because it is too jargonistic, and second, because it might contribute to the clarification of the term *history* and its various derivates, the vagueness of which is crucial to the maintenance of the myth that the term *history* designates something real.

5   The literature on "event" and "historical event" is vast. Every reflection on history ought to have event as a subject of discussion, and any reflection on history that lacks such a discussion is missing something crucial to the understanding of what "history" is all about. A useful summary of the issues involved can be found in Krzysztof Pomian's magisterial treatment of "evento" in the *Enciclopedia Einaudi*, the first chapter of his brilliant, but for some reason for the most part ignored, book *L'Ordre du temps*. The notion of "fact" as an "event under a description" comes from Danto. See also Badiou; Ricoeur; and Veyne.

6   See White, "Modernist."

7   See ch. 2. The structure-event relation is the model most favored by contemporary analysis of the event in the social sciences. See Franko; Mclean's *The Event and Its Terrors*, which has to do with the Irish famine of 1845 and afterward, an event that was known popularly as "the event" and that inspired a lot of discussion about what exactly a historical event could be; and Sewell, ch. 7, "A Theory of the Event."

8   I have not been able to confirm the existence of the term *archaiolographos* to designate an inquirer into the "origins" or remote past. The term was introduced to me by the historian Antonin Liakos, of the University of Athens, in an essay on classical Greek historical thought that is still, as far as I can tell, unpublished. I adopt it because I want to believe that implicit in the *practice* of the early Greek historians was an important distinction between the recent or proximate past and the remote or absolute past and that the former was the proper domain of what later

came to be called "historians." Bernard Williams suggests that historical inquiry is born when the remote past, formerly thought to have been inhabited by various kinds of monsters, gods, fantastic heroes, and the like, as well as men, was suddenly grasped as being inhabited by people just like ourselves and was, therefore, comprehensible by the same principles of understanding used to understand ourselves. See Williams 160–61.

9   Although many modern students of Greek culture and language have set *mythos* over against *logos* as "story" to "plot," *logos* rather than *mythos* is used by Herodotus and others when speaking about the "story" they are telling or wish to tell. In fact, many dictionaries give *mythos* for legend, fiction, or even lie (to *pseudos*) and keep *logos* for a "story" that may be imaginary or true, as the case may be. These differences allow one to keep the distinction between narration (the telling or unfolding of the story) and the narrative (the story told, its "ending" revealed, and the connection between beginning and ending established), even though the Greeks tended to run them together and see their mutual implicativeness in the making of any given "historial" account of the world.

10   To be sure, "plot" has equivalents in German (*die Handlung*) and French, Italian, and Spanish, and so on as "intrigue," "intreccio," "intriga," "trama," etc.

11   See Ankersmit's *Narrative Logic: A Semantic Analysis of the Historian's Language*, the argument of which is summarized, augmented, and contextualized in his essay "Statements, Texts, and Pictures."

12   David Carr argues that narrative forms an adequate paradigm of historical sequences because human beings in society tend to try to give order to their lives, project plans, and act in accordance with narratological life scenarios.

13   After the entry "event," under "antonyms" I found only the enigmatic instruction: "See Destiny." Turning to "Destiny.- I. Nouns," I found: "destiny, fate, lot, portion, doom, fortune, fatality, fatalism, future, future state, future existence, hereafter, next world, world to come, life to come, prospect, expectation," and, further on: "Antonyms. See Event." I asked myself in what sense "event" could ever be considered an "antonym" of "destiny." And then it dawned on me that "event" is antithetical to "destiny" in the sense that the latter connotes not only "fate" but, more generally, "ultimate outcome" of a sequence of happenings, the individual units (or parts) of which are constituted in reaction or response to "eruptions" or rather "interruptions" exogenous to the chain up to the point of their occurrence. This insight, in turn, allowed me to see the probable relation on the semantic level of event to narrative, in which, as Mink and Ricoeur have suggested, a historical event is a contingent occurrence that can be apprehended as having a place in a plot of (some) story.

14   The *ohne Eigenschaften* alludes, of course, to Musil's great novel of the modern(ist) condition that is exactly equivalent to Heidegger's notion of the "thrownness" of *Dasein* into a world without qualities. Man the wanderer, the homeless being that desires a dwelling place, is endlessly denied such a place because the world into

which he is "thrown" is made of a space in which "places" are only temporary resting points for this being-without-qualities. See Heidegger 322–25 (sect. 277–78).

15   See White, "Modernist."

16   See esp. part 3, sec. 1, "The Historical Premises." See Michel de Certeau's "The Fiction of History," in which he treats Freud's text as a novel.

17   See Oakshott, ch. 1

Works Cited

Ankersmit, F. R. *Narrative Logic: A Semantic Analysis of the Historian's Language*. Boston: Martinus Nijhoff, 1983.

——————. "Statements, Texts, and Pictures." *A New Philosophy of History*. Ed. Frank Ankersmit and Hans Kellner. London: Reaktion, 1995.

Aristotle. "On Interpretation." *The Basic Works of Aristotle*. Ed. Richard McKeon. New York: Random House, 1941. 44–61.

Badiou, Alain. *Infinite Thought: Truth and the Return of Philosophy*. Trans. Oliver Feltham and Justin Clemens. London: Continuum, 2004.

Carr, David. *Time, Narrative, and History*. Bloomington: Indiana UP, 1986.

Danto, Arthur. *Analytical Philosophy of History*. Cambridge: Harvard UP, 1965.

de Certeau, Michel. "The Fiction of History: The Writing of *Moses and Monotheism*." *The Writing of History*. Trans. Tom Conley. New York: Columbia UP, 1988. 308–54.

Franko, Mark, ed. *Ritual and Event: Interdisciplinary Perspectives*. New York: Routledge, 2007.

Freud, Sigmund. *Moses and Monotheism*. Trans. Katherine Jones. New York: Vintage, 1955.

Goody, Jack. *The Theft of History*. Cambridge: Cambridge UP, 2006.

Hacking, Ian. *Historical Ontology*. Cambridge: Harvard UP, 2002.

Heidegger, Martin. *Being and Time*. Trans. John Macquarrie and Edward Robinson. Oxford: Blackwell, 1962.

Mclean, Stuart. *The Event and Its Terrors: Ireland, Famine, Modernity*. Stanford: Stanford UP, 2004.

Nagourney, Adam. "Race and Gender Are Issues in Tense Day for Democrats." *New York Times* 14 Jan. 2008. http://www.nytimes.com/2008/01/14/us/politics/14campaign.html?scp=2&sq=January+14%2C+2008+Obama&st=nyt.

Oakshott, Michael. *On History and Other Essays*. Indianapolis: Liberty Fund, 1999.

Pomian, Krzysztof. "*Enciclopedia Einaudi*." *L'Ordre du temps*. Paris: Editions Gallimard, 1984.

Rämö, Hans. "An Aristotelian Human Time-Space Manifold: From *Chronochora* to *Kairo-topos*." *Time & Society* 8.2 (1999): 309–28.

Ricoeur, Paul. *Time and Narrative*. Vol. 1. Trans. Kathleen McLaughlin and David Pellauer. Chicago: U of Chicago P, 1984.

Roget's Thesaurus of the English Language in Dictionary Form, Being a Presentation, etc. By C. O. Sylvester Mawson. New York: Garden City, 1940.

Sahlins, Marshall. *Islands of History.* Chicago: U of Chicago P, 1985.

Sewell, William H., Jr. *Logics of History: Social Theory and Social Transformation.* Chicago: U of Chicago P, 2005.

Veyne, Paul. *Comment on écrit l'histoire suivi de Foucault révolutionne l'histoire.* Paris: Éditions du Seuil, 1978.

White, Hayden. "The Modernist Event." *Figural Realism: Studies in the Mimesis Effect.* Baltimore: Johns Hopkins UP, 1999. 66–86.

——————. "The Value of Narrativity in the Representation of Reality." *The Content of the Form: Narrative Discourse and Historical Representation.* Baltimore: Johns Hopkins UP, 1987. 1–25.

Williams, Bernard. *Truth and Truthfulness: An Essay in Genealogy.* Princeton: Princeton UP, 2002.

World History according to Katrina

*H*ow does Hurricane Katrina change our understanding of the United States, the lengths and widths of its history as well as its place in the life of the planet? As a catastrophe that casts into doubt the efficacy and security of the nation, what alternatives does it suggest, pointing to what other forms of shelter, what ways to organize human beings into meaningful groups? And how might these nonstandard groupings help us rethink the contours of the humanities, both in relation to world literature (a field already well developed) and in relation to world history, a field that perhaps still needs to be articulated, needs to be fleshed out?[1]

The nation-state seems "unbundled" by the hurricane in ways both large and small—not only as a system of defense but also as psychological insurance, political membership, and academic field. I want to use these unbundlings as an occasion to think about the circumference of our work: in terms of time frame and in terms of geographical borders. And on both fronts, it seems crucial to ask three interrelated questions. First, given the failure of the nation-state to defend its borders against a phenomenon such as Katrina, what adjustments need to be made to some

Volume 19, Number 2   DOI 10.1215/10407391-2008-007

© 2008 by Brown University and d i f f e r e n c e s : A Journal of Feminist Cultural Studies

of its assumed prerogatives, such as the claim of sovereignty? If it turns out that sovereignty, in the twenty-first century, is no longer claimable across the board, what exceptions might be made and in what contexts? And what chances are there that these shifts would reorient the practice of democracy itself, taking it out of its traditional mold and freeing it to address new issues, including the long-term relation between human rights and the world's climate?

It is instructive to begin with an essay on Katrina by Michael Ignatieff, published on September 25, 2005 in the *New York Times Magazine*. "When the levees broke, the contract of American citizenship failed," Ignatieff says. The breach is not just in the physical structures, or in New Orleans as a physical city, but in something even more consequential, namely, the integrity of the United States as a nation, its ability to *be* sovereign. According to Ignatieff, the most "basic term" of this sovereignty is "protection: helping citizens to protect their families and possessions from forces beyond their control." And, just as the nation is defined by its power to protect, citizens are defined by their right to demand that protection. They are "entitled to this because they are Americans." Nationality, in other words, ought to be synonymous with a guaranteed safety, an insulation from any harm that arises. It ought to be our bulwark against the storm. And the tragedy of Katrina is that it seems to have thrown that bulwark into question. Ignatieff summarizes the problem as follows:

> *In America, a levee defends a foundational moral intuition: all lives are worth protecting and, because this is America, worth protecting at the highest standard. This principle was betrayed by the Army Corps of Engineers, by the state and local officials who knew the levees needed repair and did nothing, and by Congress, which allowed the president to cut appropriations for levee renewal.*

According to this analysis, the problem is that the sovereignty of the nation has not been sovereign enough. The United States ought to have been an invincible line of defense, and it was not. The remedy, then, is also fairly simple: that line has to be firmed up, made invincible once again. The narrative that Ignatieff constructs begins and ends with the levees for this reason, because not only is the nation-state broken and then mended on their backs but to see the problem as solely a problem of the levees is already to predetermine the solution, making Katrina an event internal to the United States, an engineering failure, something that can be fixed without changing our basic sense of what the sovereign nation amounts to, what it is equipped (or not equipped) to do, and the extent of protection it is able to offer its citizens.

Nonsovereign History

As must be clear, I find this approach unduly limiting. I would like to explore a larger set of analytic coordinates than those suggested by Ignatieff and to do so in a slightly roundabout fashion, by way of a debate that casts doubt on the sovereign claim of the nation, especially its adequacy as a unit of time, a debate that has galvanized historians no less than literary scholars. James Sheehan, in his 2006 presidential address to the American Historical Association, specifically raises this as an issue. It would "be foolish to deny the importance of states," Sheehan says, "but the state was not and is not history's natural telos. The emergence of states was neither inevitable nor uniform nor irreversible" (1–2).[2] Even though national chronology might look like the only chronology there is, a self-evident way of measuring time, we pay a steep price when we reify it and routinize it, allowing ourselves no other frame of reference. "Modern historiography is inextricably linked with the modern nation," Thomas Bender writes. "This has both given focus to historical inquiry and won for it a place in civic life. But it has also been disabling, silencing stories both smaller and larger than the nation" (vii). As a unit of time, the nation tends to work as a pair of evidentiary shutters, blocking out all those phenomena that do not fit into its intervals, reducing to nonevents all those processes either too large or too small to show up on its watch. Prasenjit Duara, historian of China—a country with a long record of just such disappearing acts—urges us to "rescue history from the nation" for just that reason. To make sovereign borders the limits for data gathering is to make it a foregone conclusion that the form of the nation is the only form that matters.[3] It is to take that form and reproduce it in the form of the discipline, "naturalizing the nation-state as the skin that contains the experience of the past" (Duara, "Transnationalism" 25).

That skin is very much the skin for those of us who call ourselves Americanists. To be sure, much of our work is critical of the nation. Still, the very existence of an "Americanist" field implicitly (and sometimes explicitly) reinforces the idea that an autonomous body of evidence can be derived from the United States, with clear dividing lines that separate it from other bodies of evidence. Neither American history nor American literature would have been a field without this assumption. Territorial sovereignty is foundational to both in this sense: not only does it produce a database that legitimizes the field, it also institutes a cutoff line for what falls outside. As Anthony Giddens observes in a different context, "Sovereignty provides an ordering principle for what is 'internal' to states and what is 'external' to them" (281). The concept of "off limits" inversely defines the borders of a political jurisdiction; it also inversely defines the borders of a field of knowledge.[4]

This conflation of nation and field leads to a research agenda almost tautological: to study the United States, we need go no further than the United States. This makes things easier, though not everyone would agree that such a tautology is in fact valid, a good approximation of the forces that shape the world. Janice Radway, in her presidential address to the American Studies Association in 1998, makes a point of invoking this model—and rejecting it. In language strikingly similar to Duara's, she cautions us against any conception of the field as being like the territorial nation, lined with a skin:

> [F]ar from being conceived on the model of a container—that is, as a particular kind of hollowed out object with evident edges or skin enclosing certain organically uniform contents—territories and geographies need to be reconceived as spatially situated and intricately intertwined networks of social relationships. (15)

Radway's challenge to the "container" model turns the study of the United States from a closed space to an open network, with no sovereign borders, nothing that will keep it defensibly separated from the rest of the world. What does this mean in practice? Well, for one thing, we cannot say, with any degree of finality, that anything is "extraneous," because extraneousness is not an attribute that is cut-and-dried, antecedently given. It is a happenstance, a contextual variable, changing with the array of forces that happen to be in play, and with their different modes of interaction. This lack of intrinsic separation suggests that the analytic domain is always going to be heuristically stretched beyond any set of prescribed coordinates. The study of the United States can never be tautologically identical to the borders of the United States, because it can never keep the "outside" a permanent outside, externalized by defensible borders. The field then, according to Radway, can bear no resemblance to the territorial form of the nation. The nation is sovereign, or imagines itself to be. The field can have no such pretension.

What does it mean to write a history that is nonsovereign, with the seemingly extraneous being always ready, at a moment's notice, to morph into the un-extraneous? I would like to come back to Katrina as a test case and explore two instances of this dynamic, when a seemingly secure jurisdiction suddenly bursts at the seams, becoming a kind of flooded container, flooded by an outside that refuses to stay out. To explore these two scenarios, I would like, first, to follow the unconventional coverage of Katrina by a local newspaper, the New Orleans *Times-Picayune*. The *Times-Picayune* received the Pulitzer Prize for this report, so the importance of its work has certainly been recognized. But the history that it gives us is a nonsovereign history, not only because the initiative is coming from the ground up, from a local newspaper, rather than reflecting a national consensus, but also because this initiative produces a database that in no way matches the official borders of the United States. Nonsovereign history is offbeat, off-key, off-center. Its unorthodox paths jump from the micro to the macro and bypass the default center, going over and under the jurisdiction of the nation. Its scale is both smaller and larger: operating subnationally, on the one hand, as a grassroots phenomenon and transnationally, on the other, as a cross-border phenomenon, and, in this way, bringing into relief a practice of democracy significantly different from the nation-bound variety, at once dispersed and energized by a multicentric input network.

Cross-Stitching Time

What the New Orleans *Times-Picayune* does, specifically, is to send its own staff writer, John McQuaid, to a different country—the Netherlands—in order to broaden the evidentiary base, gathering information wherever relevant, tracing a series of zig-zags between two continents, two analytic poles. These zig-zags generate a cross-stitching of time, necessary because the United States is not the only country in the world having to deal with storms and the flooding that comes with those storms. The Netherlands, throughout its history, has been facing this problem, and its collective decisions shed light on the United States for just that reason. What we will eventually see, in the robustness and thoroughness of the Dutch response, is an alternative time line, a trajectory of action at once local and national, an instance of democratic politics that would have been helpful if, indeed, it had "flooded" the United States, if, indeed, its cross-currents had permeated these shores.

"The North Sea's furious winters can kick up storm surges more than 13 feet high—a lethal threat to a country where millions live below sea level, some as much as 22 feet down," John McQuaid notes. On February 1, 1953, the Netherlands was hit by a North Sea storm that lasted thirty-three hours. The storm surge—water pushed to the shore by the winds—was 150 inches higher than the normal sea level. The dikes collapsed in more than 450 places. Over 1,800 people died; some 4,000 buildings were swept away or badly damaged (Moore). Out of a population of around twelve million, 100,000 had to evacuate. Twice as many people were killed by the flood as by the German bombing of Rotterdam in 1940.

The scale of the destruction is very much comparable to New Orleans, and the preceding circumstances are also quite similar. Simon Rozendaal, a Dutch journalist writing in the *Wall Street Journal*, comments expressly on this. "As in the American Gulf states, the Dutch levee system had been neglected. It was not long after World War II: the Netherlands had just lost its colony, Indonesia; and the Cold War diverted money and attention." Local disasters are, in this sense, the almost predictable side effects of global geopolitics. They are part of a larger distributive pattern—a pattern of unequal protection that Ulrich Beck calls the global "risk society"—with the risk falling on the least privileged and being maximized at just those points where the resources have been most depleted.[5] This was true of the Netherlands; it was true of New Orleans. In both cases, the military budget was funded at the expense of domestic infrastructures, paving the way for their eventual breakdown. The Lake Pontchartrain and Vicinity Hurricane Protection project, a public works project aimed at building up levees and protecting pumping stations on the east bank of the Mississippi in Orleans, St. Bernard, St. Charles, and Jefferson parishes, received less than 20 percent of the funding requested by the Army Corps of Engineers. This was not a secret; it was already public knowledge back in 2004. The *Philadelphia Inquirer* had run a story about this, reporting that it "appears that the money has been moved in the president's budget to handle homeland security and the war in Iraq" (qtd. in Dyson 81).

The *Philadelphia Inquirer* and the New Orleans *Times-Picayune* are helpless witnesses—to a time frame waved aside, dismissed as unimportant. In the unfolding catastrophe, they have the status of a tragic chorus. They come bearing knowledge, and they go nowhere. They, along with various science magazines, have been writing reports for years—useless reports—about various warning signs: the erosion of the wetlands, the subsidence of the soil, and the presence of dangerous chemicals as well as dangerous artificial waterways such as the MRGO (the Mississippi River Gulf Outlet), which greatly increase the power of the storm surge. These warnings had absolutely no effect on government policies: this was true not only in the United States but also in the Netherlands. Six months before the 1953 disaster, the Dutch engineer Johan van Veen had calculated that the storm surge could rise up to thirteen feet relative to the sinking coast. The Dutch meteorological service made the same prediction, but only three of the one thousand water boards, which managed the dikes, had a subscription to this service (Rozendaal). In the case of New Orleans, the warnings had come from FEMA's own modeling of a hypothetical Hurricane Pam in 2004 and from dire forecasts appearing in *Scientific American*, *National Geographic*, *Popular Mechanics*, the *Times-Picayune*, the *Houston Chronicle*, the *New York Times*, as well as on the PBS science program *Nova* (Dyson 77–86). But all this information came to nothing. It was not able to percolate to a higher level, not able to lead to the dismantling of the MRGO, for instance, or to the rediversion of funds from Iraq back to these domestic projects. And it most certainly was not able to reverse the unequal protection endemic in this country. Parallel to the physical levees that are in disrepair, there seems to be an invisible system of levees that work all too well: shutting out all local input and turning public policy into a closed-door affair, a strictly bureaucratic decision.

Dutch Delta Works

So far, then, a cross-stitching of time seems to show only the same pattern: a common hazard and a common failure of the democratic process itself, a kind of blockage between available information and government action. But here the symmetry ends. Flood protection in the Netherlands after 1953 diverges sharply from the United States, suggesting also that the Dutch democracy is now structurally very different from its American counterpart. It is this alternative thread of time that the New Orleans *Times-Picayune* tries to highlight by sending its staff reporter there.

Before 1953, the Dutch had tried to protect their settlements by canals lined with dikes, essentially the same as the levee system in south Louisiana. The 1953 flood revealed a major flaw in that strategy, a flaw that would now prove fatal for New Orleans. Levee-lined canals, it turns out, are fundamentally unsafe: during severe storms, they would themselves become deadly passageways, allowing the churning ocean to penetrate far inland. After Katrina, a team of Dutch engineers went to New Orleans to study the failed system, and they repeated their previous reservations about the overreliance on levees. The Dutch engineer Jurgen Battjes points out:

> *The region's levee-lined canals were conduits for Katrina's storm surge to pour into the heart of the city. From the east, water flowed into the Intercoastal Waterway and Industrial Canal, where floodwalls were topped and then collapsed, flooding the Lower Ninth Ward, St. Bernard Parish and eastern New Orleans. From Lake Pontchartrain, it flowed into the 17th Street and London Avenue drainage canals, which were breached, flooding central New Orleans. (qtd. in McQuaid)*

The Dutch Delta Works (Deltawerken), begun shortly after 1953, adopted a different strategy. Rather than building higher and stronger dikes along the canals, as they had always done, the Dutch opted instead to construct giant barriers across all ocean inlets, sealing off the estuaries, and turning them into giant freshwater lakes. The first (in the Hollandse IJssel) went into operation in 1958. This was followed by the damming of the Veerse Gat and the Zandkreek in 1961, the Haringvliet and the Brouwershavensche Gat in 1971 and 1972. These closures blocked off the invading ocean, but they also destroyed the unique ecosystem of the estuaries, a unique mix of freshwater and seawater, and the breeding ground for many species of North Sea fish. Environmentalists as well as mussel and oyster fishermen fiercely opposed the plan for just that reason (Dutch).

From the 1970s on, then, the philosophy behind the Delta Works would undergo yet another shift, this time taking into account a twofold understanding of "protection," equalizing it across the entire habitat and respecting the input from local communities. The goal was not only to protect southwestern Holland against the storm surge of the North Sea but also to protect the existing ecosystem of the river estuaries. The enormous Oosterscheldt Barrier was the result. One of the most spectacular feats of hydraulic engineering in the world, this barrier is 5.6 miles long, with sixty-two moveable flood gates, each the size of a twelve-story apartment building. This was followed by the equally immense Maeslant Barrier, which opened in 1997. These massive public works projects are the outcomes of active intervention by the Dutch citizenry. They are designed to give the Netherlands a macro policy that reflects local input, a level of protection adequate to a flood that would come once every 10,000 years (Dutch).

The technology is certainly impressive, but even more so is the broad-based democratic process that puts it to work. Flood protection in the Netherlands—as government policy and as community effort—is accompanied by public debate every step of the way. It was this local input that led to the change in direction in the 1970s. And it was this local input, multiplied manifold, that made it possible for this small nation to commit itself to these vast expenditures and to plan ahead in terms of a statistical time frame of 10,000 years. More recently, in preparation for the sea-level rise that is a foreseeable though not-yet-realized consequence of global warming, the Netherlands has planned still further ahead, implementing a new policy called "Make Room for the River," moving populations away from some areas that, in the future, will most certainly be flooded (Palca). Democracy, in the Dutch context, means at least three things: public information available to everyone; local input having a direct impact on policy decisions; and a political will to limit vulnerability across the board, extending protection to populations both human and not human, both currently voting and not yet born.

Against the small details as well as the long-term planning of that democratic culture, what happens in the United States must be called something else. To begin with, the New Orleans levees were designed to protect only against a storm that would come once every fifty years—in other words, only against a Category 3 hurricane. And even this modest level of protection was not always maintained, as Ivor van Heerden, deputy director of the Louisiana State University Hurricane Center, points out.[6] In its self-study released on June 1, 2006, the Army Corps of Engineers admits to this, accepting blame not only for the flawed design and construction of the levees but also for its underestimation of hurricane strength based on outdated standards (Schwartz). This is a problem it has known for some time. "It's possible to protect New Orleans from a Category 5 hurricane," Al Naomi, senior project manager for the Corps, told the *Philadelphia Inquirer* on October 8, 2004. "But we've got to start. To do nothing is tantamount to negligence." The Corps submitted a proposal that year to Congress requesting $4 million to fund a preliminary study. Congress tabled the proposal, never bringing it to the floor, citing budgetary constraints resulting from the Iraq War (qtd. in Nussbaum).

Unlike the robust input from Dutch communities, decisions in the United States were made—or not made—behind closed doors, by a legislative body acting only out of fiscal concerns, without ever opening up its reasoning to public scrutiny. Still, even if that public scrutiny had taken place, it is not clear that the Dutch time scale of the "10,000-year flood" would have been adopted. Long-term planning has never had much of a place on the federal, state, or municipal agenda: 10,000 years seem almost unimaginable. As the *Washington Post* reports:

> *In 1982, the Orleans Levee District urged the Corps to "lower its design standards to provide more realistic hurricane protec-tion." The levee district, stocked with political appointees, could spend freely on private investigators, riverboat gambling, and a $2.4 million Mardi Gras foundation. But it said it could not afford its share of protection from a 200-year storm, suggesting that 100-year protection would be fine. ("Slow")*

This strange sense of proportions might turn out to be one of the most destructive effects of the time scale of a young nation, one that allows nei-ther a long past nor a long future to interfere with the short but oversized centrality of the present. What does it mean never to think of time except in single and double digits? And how might these single and double digits affect a nation's ability to deal with events such as hurricanes, whose poten-tial for harm outstrips those digits by many orders of magnitude? A nonsov-ereign history of Katrina shows that, beyond the broken levees, what needs to be mended is the democratic process itself and its need for a reference frame beyond the geography and chronology of the nation. The example of the Netherlands is *not* extraneous to the United States for just that reason. Indeed, it is only by not externalizing this body of evidence—not blocking it out, not seeing it as foreign or exotic—that we can begin to circumvent the short time line of the United States, embracing a democratic practice centered not on this nation, but taking its circumference from the world.

The World's Water

That circumference, in turn, radically changes the way we think about causality: the web that articulates it, the claims that can be pressed, and the responses needed as a result. The implications are far reaching, because to draw a larger input circle around the nation is also to draw a larger circle of accountability, to give a broad interpretation to the harm that it might have perpetrated at a distance, harm that might seem extraneous from one point of view. How, for instance, can we make a nation face up to the death and destruction that it is causing hundreds and thousands of civilians, thousands of miles away, on a different continent? Justice looks very different when it is framed in this way, seen as extended rather than encapsulated. Rather than being a problem of crime and punishment contained within a single nation, it becomes another instance of the flooded container: flooded, in this case, by the causal web that links it, against the illusion of sovereignty, to cross-currents affecting the entire planet, a seascape turbulent and borderless.

World history and world literature have much to contribute to this enlarged sense of justice, for crucial to these fields are just such cross-currents, input networks with multiple sources, fluid rather than territorial. Hurricanes are very much part of this seascape: they are indexes to the hydrology of the world as a whole. Generated by air-sea interaction, this hydrology can be adequately studied only through "multi-basin indices," which is to say, by comparing data from the North Pacific, Indian, Southwest Pacific, and North Atlantic Oceans. Not only are hurricanes water-borne disasters, they are disasters unique to warm water: as long as the sea surface temperature remains below 26.5 degrees Celsius (80 degrees Fahrenheit), no hurricane will form. When oceans get heated up, they fuel a convection process that transforms cold-core tropical depressions into hot-core cyclones. Katrina itself strengthened to a Category 5 hurricane when it was passing over the Gulf of Mexico, where the surface waters were unusually warm, about 2 degrees Fahrenheit warmer than normal for that time of year (Pew Center).[7]

Sea surface temperature is the single most important factor in hurricane formation. And it was by looking at this data that the MIT climatologist, Kerry Emanuel, was able to predict what was to come. On July 31, 2005, one month before Katrina, Emanuel published his research in the online edition of the journal *Nature*. Tracking hurricanes by their "power dissipation index" (a combination of the lifetime of storms and their intensity), Emanuel shows that "this index has increased markedly since the mid-1970s," an upward trend strongly correlated with the rise in the sea surface temperature. Both the duration of hurricanes and their wind speeds have "doubled in the past 30 years" as the Pacific and the Atlantic have warmed by 1 degree Fahrenheit between 1970 and 2004. Since changing ocean temperatures are themselves indices to climate change, Emanuel sees the increasingly destructive hurricanes as "at least partly anthropogenic." He predicts "a substantial increase in hurricane-related losses in the 21st century" (Emanuel).

Emanuel's study was corroborated almost immediately in a parallel study by a team from the Georgia Institute of Technology, reported in *Science* on September 16, 2005. By looking at "the number of tropical cyclones and cyclone days as well as tropical cyclone intensity over the past 35 years, in an environment of increasing sea surface temperature," this study finds that "hurricanes in the strongest categories (4 + 5) have almost doubled in number [. . .]. These changes occur in all of the ocean basins." How to explain this across-the-board jump? J. B. Webster, speaking for the Georgia Tech team, is even less ambiguous in seeing a strong correlation between the rising ocean temperatures and the rising concentrations of atmospheric carbon dioxide—chief of the greenhouse gases—though they concede that "attribution of 30-year trends to global warming would require a longer global data record and, especially, a deeper understanding of the role of hurricanes in the general circulation of the atmosphere and ocean" (Webster et al.).

Whether or not hurricanes can be directly traced to global warming,[8] what seems clear is that the database needs to be planetary in scope, studying all the oceans in conjunction. Studied in conjunction, they point to a changing world, becoming daily less hospitable, looking less and less like the planet that has supported our species and other species. We take it so much for granted that we never notice that its features have grown ominous. Of the weapons of mass destruction already lined up, the most deadly will probably come not in the form of hurricanes, but as a simpler hydrology, one less spectacular though infinitely more catastrophic: namely, the rising sea levels due to the melting of the Arctic and Antarctic ice sheets.

In its 2001 report, the United Nations's Intergovernmental Panel on Climate Change (IPCC) predicted that sea-level rise in the twenty-first century will proceed "at an average rate of 2.2 to 4.4 times the rate over the 20th century," while singling out the West Antarctic ice sheet as especially worrisome, since it "contains enough ice to raise sea level by 6 meters" (Houghton et al. 642). Meanwhile, seismic stations revealed a significant increase in "icequakes," caused by ice sheets breaking loose and lurching forward; the annual number of these icequakes registering 4.6 or greater on the Richter scale doubled from seven to fourteen in the late 1990s, and it doubled again by 2005. Satellite measurements of the earth's gravitational field showed a loss of fifty cubic miles of ice in Greenland in 2005, matched by a similar loss in West Antarctica (Hansen 13). The new IPCC report, issued in February 2007, stuck to a more conservative figure for the sea-level rise (7.8 inches to 2 feet by the century's end), but the human cost is staggering even at this rate (Intergovernmental).[9] The World Bank estimates, for instance, that even a three-foot rise in sea level would turn at least 60 million people into refugees (Eilperin).

What would the United States look like? The fate of New Orleans would have been sealed long before then, as would the fate of many other coastal cities. Al Gore, in *An Inconvenient Truth*, gives us a computer projection of what would be left of Florida if the sea level were to increase by eighteen to twenty feet; it is a horrendous image. The century ahead will most certainly be dominated by this advancing seascape as the earth continues to heat up. Sovereign borders will be so diluted—literally—that they will be small comfort for u.s. citizens; even the world's largest military budget will not yield a credible line of defense. Yet, the irony is that, while the nation can provide no long-term protection, it is quite capable of action that has the potential for long-term harm. The balance between human history and nonhuman processes, always problematic, is now weighted more and more in the latter's direction, with a growing gap between the kind of habitat the human species has depended on and the kind of habitat the planet is becoming. The United States is ill prepared for this development, though there are signs now that the tide might be turning, that climate change might be reeducating all of us in the primacy of the planet over the sovereignty of any nation. At this critical moment, it is especially important for the humanities to rethink its space and time coordinates, to take up questions that might once have seemed far removed—coming not only from hitherto extraneous fields such as earth and planetary sciences, but also from hitherto extraneous populations not traditionally included in the discipline.

Arctic Time Line

One such population is the Inuit living in the Arctic Circle. It is here that global warming is felt most directly and most severely, since the threshold for catastrophic change is much lower at the two poles: the difference of one or two degrees can have drastic consequences for the glaciers and the ice sheets. When it comes to climate change, the Arctic is ahead of the rest of the world: it has a time line of its own. In December 1995, the ipcc issued a landmark report noting this uneven development. This was reaffirmed in 2004 by the eight-nation Arctic Climate Impact Assessment, which concluded that the Arctic is experiencing "some of the most rapid and severe climate change on earth" (Abstract) In *An Inconvenient Truth* this is dramatized as the plight of the polar bear, and what makes the world unlivable for the polar bear also makes it unrecognizable for the Inuit. They have a word for it, *uggianaqtuq*, referring to the weather, a "familiar friend now behaving strangely" (UNESCO). In November 2000, the Inuit released a forty-five-minute video to document this fatal alienation. Entitled *Sila Alangotok: Inuit Observations on Climate Change*, it offers an extensive record of melting ice, eroding coastlines, and the appearance of wildlife never seen before, including the Pacific salmon and the robin.[10] It is this unrecognizability of the world, the unrecognizability of their habitat, that makes it necessary for the Inuit Circumpolar Conference (a federation made up 150,000 native peoples in Canada, Greenland, Russia, and the United States) to seek legal action against the world's foremost emitter of greenhouse gases.

This is not easy to do. Currently, the infrastructure for transnational legal action is still very sketchy. Just as we do not have the legal instrumentalities to prosecute nations for the long-distance military harm they incur, neither do we have the legal instrumentalities to prosecute nations for the long-distance environmental harm they perpetrate. We do, of course, have courts that operate on a transnational level. There are four of these at the moment: the International Court of Justice at the Hague; the International Criminal Court, also at the Hague; the Court of Justice of the European Communities at Luxembourg; and the European Court of Human Rights at Strasbourg. The first of these, the International Court of Justice, created in 1945, will hear only cases brought before it by nation-states.[11] The other three courts do in fact hear cases brought by nonstate actors,[12] but the grievance of the Inuit does not rise to the level of the International Criminal Court, and, not being a member of the European Union, its case also cannot be heard in the two European courts. However, with the help of environmental groups such as Earth Justice and the Center for International Environmental Law, the Inuit were able to file a petition against the Bush administration with the Inter-American Commission on Human Rights on December 7, 2005, "seeking relief from violations resulting from global warming caused by acts and omissions of the United States" (Inuit Circumpolar Council).

Almost all the deteriorating conditions of the Arctic can be traced to climate change, not only changes in the "quality, quantity and timing of snowfall" but also the destruction of coastal communities through the increasingly erratic behavior of water in all its forms:

Permafrost, which holds together unstable underground gravel and inhibits water drainage, is melting at an alarming rate, causing slumping, landslides, severe erosion and loss of ground moisture, wetlands and lakes. The loss of sea ice, which dampens the impact of storms on coastal areas, has resulted in increasingly violent storms hitting the coastline, exacerbating erosion and flooding. Erosion in turn exposes coastal permafrost to warmer air and water, resulting in faster permafrost melts. These transformations have had a devastating impact on some coastal communities, particularly in Alaska and the Canadian Beaufort Sea Region [. . .]. Other factors have also affected water levels. Changes in precipitation and temperature have led to sudden spring thaws that release large amounts of water, flooding rivers and eroding their streambeds. Yet, after spring floods, rivers and lakes are left with unusually low levels of water, further diminished by increased evaporation during the longer summer. These changes affect the availability and quality of natural drinking water sources. The fish stocks upon which Inuit rely are profoundly affected by changing water levels. Fish sometimes cannot reach their spawning grounds, their eggs are exposed or washed ashore, or northward moving species compete with the native stocks for ecological niches. (Inuit Circumpolar Council)

Violent storms, floods, soil erosion, loss of wetlands—these are problems we associate with New Orleans and the Gulf of Mexico. It should not come as too much of a surprise, though, to see them also played out, thousands of miles away, in the Arctic Ocean, since there is, in fact, no dividing line separating these two bodies of water. This single, criss-crossing, and already damaged hydrology makes it clear that climate, geology, and human and nonhuman life are all complexly intertwined, part of the same fluid continuum. The catastrophe, already writ large in this seemingly remote part of the world, is closer to us than we think. Sheila Watt-Cloutier, chair of the Inuit Circumpolar Conference, received the United Nations Lifetime Achievement Award for Human Development and, along with Al Gore, was nominated for the 2007 Nobel Peace Prize. The Inter-American Commission on Human Rights began its hearings on climate change in March 2007. While the commission has no power of enforcement, a finding in favor of the Inuit could be the basis for future lawsuits in u.s. federal courts. World history here takes on its exemplary form, calling our attention to the tangled fate of the planet, and urging us toward an enlarged sense of democracy, an enlarged sense of justice. This enlargement can begin only with local knowledge, with micro evidence and bottom-up chronologies. If these space and time coordinates look unfamiliar, perhaps the study of the United States needs to become unfamiliar to itself in just this way.

WAI CHEE DIMOCK is the William Lampson Professor of English and American Studies at Yale University. She is the author, most recently, of *Through Other Continents: American Literature across Deep Time* (Princeton University Press, 2006) and coeditor, with Lawrence Buell, of *Shades of the Planet: American Literature as World Literature* (Princeton University Press, 2007).

Notes

1　For two efforts in this direction, one general and one specific, see Colley; and McNeill and McNeill.

2　For other well-known critiques of the nation-state, see Gellner; Hobsbawm; and Renan.

3　For an important critique of the nation-form, see Balibar, "Nation" and "Racism."

4　For a sustained argument linking sovereignty to the conditions of knowledge, see Bartelson.

5　See also Bullard; Cutter; Kasperson and Kasperson.

6　According to van Heerden, the levees could actually offer protection only against a Category 2 storm, with wind speeds of up to 110 miles an hour. See "Levees Rebuilt." See also van Heerden.

7　Katrina weakened to Category 4 shortly before landfall in Louisiana and Mississippi.

8　Scientists who disagree with Emanuel and Webster think that the more destructive hurricanes are caused not by global warming but by a natural cycle called "multi-decadal oscillations." For a summary and documentation of the debate, see "Global."

9　For a good summary of the report, see McKibben.

10　A BBC report gives a good account of the video. See "Climate Change in the Canadian Arctic." See also Inuit Circumpolar Council, "Responding to the Global Climate Change."

11　The International Court of Justice (ICJ) was created in 1945 under the Charter of the United Nations. See http://www.icj-cij.org/ icjwww/generalinformation/ ibbook/Bbookframepage.htm.

12　The Court of Justice of the European Communities, the legal institution of the European Union, whose charge is to enforce "community law [. . .] separate from, yet superior to national law," was initially created under the Treaties of Paris and Rome in 1952. See http://curia.europa.eu/en/instit/ presentationfr/index_cje.htm. The European Court of Human Rights (ECHR), the judicial arm of the Council of Europe, started out as the Convention for the Protection of Human Rights and Fundamental Freedoms (1950) and became consolidated as a single, full-time court on November 1, 1998. The International Criminal Court (ICC) was established

on July 17, 1998, when 120 states
adopted the Statute of Rome. The
statute provides for its entry into
effect sixty days after sixty states

have ratified it, which happened
on April 11, 2002. Accordingly,
the ICC went into effect on July 1,
2002.

Works Cited

Balibar, Étienne. "The Nation Form: History and Ideology." Balibar and Wallerstein 86–106.

———. "Racism and Nationalism." Balibar and Wallerstein 37–68.

Balibar, Étienne, and Immanuel Wallerstein. *Race, Nation, Class: Ambiguous Identities.* London: Verso, 1991.

Bartelson, Jens. *A Genealogy of Sovereignty.* Cambridge: Cambridge UP, 1995.

Beck, Ulrich. *Risk Society: Towards a New Modernity.* London: Sage, 1992.

Bender, Thomas. Preface. Bender vii–ix.

Bender, Thomas, ed. *Rethinking American History in a Global Age.* Berkeley: U of California P, 2002.

Bullard, Richard D., ed. *Unequal Protection: Environmental Justice and Communities of Color.* San Francisco: Sierra Club Books, 1994.

"Climate Change in the Canadian Arctic." BBC. http://bbc.co.uk/worldservice/sci_tech/highlights/010510_canadianarctic.shtml.

Colley, Linda. *The Ordeal of Elizabeth Marsh: A Woman in World History.* New York: Pantheon, 2007.

Cutter, Susan L. *Hazards, Vulnerability, and Environmental Justice.* London: Earthscan, 2006.

Duara, Prasenjit. *Rescuing History from the Nation: Questioning Narratives of Modern China.* Chicago: U of Chicago P, 1995.

———. "Transnationalism and the Challenge to National Histories." Bender 25–46.

Dutch Ministerie van Buitelandse Zaken. "The Dutch Struggle against the Waters." http://www.thehollandring.com/1953-ramp.shtml.

Dyson, Michael Eric. *Come Hell or High Water: Hurricane Katrina and the Color of Disaster.* New York: Basic Civitas, 2006.

Eilperin, Juliet. "Clues to Rising Seas Are Hidden in Polar Ice." *Washington Post* 16 July 2007: A6.

Emanuel, Kerry. "Increasing Destructiveness of Tropical Cyclones over the Past 30 Years." *Nature* 31 July 2005. http://www.nature.com/nature/journal/vaop/ncurrent/full/nature03906.html.

Gellner, Ernest. *Nations and Nationalism.* Oxford: Oxford UP, 1983.

Giddens, Anthony. *The Nation-State and Violence.* Berkeley: U of California P, 1987.

"Global Warming and Hurricanes." Geophysical Fluid Dynamics Laboratory at the National Oceanic and Atmospheric Administration. http://www.gfdl.noaa.gov/~tk/glob_warm_hurr.html.

Hansen, Jim. "The Threat to the Planet." *New York Review of Books* 13 July 2006: 12–16.

Hobsbawm, Eric. *Nations and Nationalism since 1780*. Cambridge: Cambridge UP, 1990.

Houghton, J. H., et al., eds. *Climate Change 2001: The Scientific Basis: Contribution of Working Group to the Third Assessment Report of the Intergovernmental Panel on Climate Change*. New York: Cambridge UP, 2001.

Ignatieff, Michael. "The Broken Contract." *New York Times Magazine* 25 Sept. 2005. http://www.nytimes.com/2005/09/25/magazine/25wwln.html?scp=1&sq=The+Broken+Contract+Ignatieff&st=nyt.

An Inconvenient Truth. Dir. Davis Guggenheim. Lawrence Bender Productions, 2006.

Intergovernmental Panel on Climate Change (IPCC). *Arctic Climate Assessment Report*. Cambridge: Cambridge UP, 2004.

———. *Climate Change 2007: The Physical Science Basis: Summary for Policy Makers. Contribution of Working Group I to the Fourth Assessment Report of the Intergovernmental Panel on Climate Change*. Feb. 2007. http://www.usgcrp.gov/usgcrp/links/ipcc.htm#4wg1.

Inuit Circumpolar Council. "Inuit Petition Inter-American Commission on Human Rights to Oppose Climate Change Caused by the United States of America." *Inuit*. http://www.inuitcircumpolar.com//index.php?ID=316&Lang=En.

———. "Responding to the Global Climate Change: The Perspective of the Inuit Circumpolar Conference on the Arctic Climate Impact Assessment." http://inuitcircumpolar.com/index.php?ID=267&Lang=En.

Kasperson, Jeanne X., and Roger Kasperson, eds. *Global Environmental Risk*. Tokyo: United Nations, 2001.

"Levees Rebuilt Just in Time, but Doubts Remain." *New York Times* 25 May 2006. www.nytimes.com/2006/05/25/us/25flood.html.

McKibben, Bill. "Warning on Warming." *New York Review of Books* 15 Mar. 2007: 44–45.

McNeill, John, and William McNeill. *The Human Web: A Bird's-Eye View of World History*. New York: Norton, 2003.

McQuaid, John. "Beating Back the Sea: How the Dutch Fight to Save Their Low-Lying Land." *Times-Picayune* 13 Nov. 2005: A1.

Moore, Molly. "Rethinking Defenses against Sea's Power." *Washington Post* 8 Sept. 2005: A22.

Nussbaum, Paul. "New Orleans' Growing Danger." *Philadelphia Inquirer* 4 Oct. 2004. http://hurricane.lsu.edu/_in_the_news/phillyinquirer100804.htm.

Palca, Joe. "In a Strategic Reversal, Dutch Embrace Floods." NPR. *Morning Edition* 22 Jan. 2008.

Pew Center on Global Climate Change. "Was Katrina's Power a Product of Global Warming?" Sept. 2005. http://pewclimate.org/specialreports/katrina.cfm.

Radway, Janice. "What's in a Name? Presidential Address to the American Studies Association." 20 Nov. 1998. *American Quarterly* 51 (Mar. 1999): 1–32.

Renan, Ernest. "What Is a Nation?" *Nation and Narration*. Ed. Homi K. Bhabha. New York: Routledge, 1990. 8–22.

Rozendaal, Simon. "Katrina, Juliana, and Wilhelmina." *Wall Street Journal* 7 Sept. 2005: A16.

Schwartz, John. "Army Builders Accept Blame over Flooding." *New York Times* 2 June 2006. www.nytimes.com/2006/06/02/us/nationalspecial/02corps.html.

Sheehan, James J. "Presidential Address: The Problem of Sovereignty in European History." *American Historical Review* 111 (Feb. 2006): 1–15.

Sila Alangotok: Inuit Observations on Climate Change. International Institute for Sustainable Development. 2000.

"The Slow Drowning of New Orleans." *Washington Post* 9 Oct. 2005: A1.

unesco. "The Inuit, First Witnesses of Climate Changes." unesco. New Courier. Nov. 2005. http://portal.unesco.org/en/ev.php-URL_ID=30532&URL_DO=DO_TOPIC&URL_SECTION=201.html.

van Heerden, Ivor. *The Storm: What Went Wrong during Hurricane Katrina: Inside Story from a Louisiana Scientist*. New York: Viking, 2006.

Webster, P. J., et al. "Changes in Tropical Cyclone Number, Duration, and Intensity in a Warming Environment." *Science* 16 Sept. 2005. http://www.sciencemag.org/cgi/content/full/309/5742/1844.

JONATHAN ELMER

Babo's Razor; or, Discerning the Event in an Age of Differences

*H*ow can he be so stupid? How can he fail to see that, when the Ashantee clang their hatchets together, this is a threat, not an amusement? Does he not realize that the servant's open razor hesitates at the fainting captain's neck not from solicitude but in a conscious crystallization of menace? In Herman Melville's *Benito Cereno* (1855), the American captain Amasa Delano happens upon the *San Dominick* drifting without apparent purpose off the coast of Chile, a ship ostensibly commanded by one Benito Cereno, with whom Delano holds a series of bizarre conversations in the company of Cereno's slave and servant, Babo. The ship is a place of mystery, confusion, and foreboding for Delano, but he dispels all his doubts about what is going on until Cereno jumps wildly into his departing boat, at which moment the slaves reveal themselves to be in "ferocious piratical revolt" (734). A postscript consisting of selections from trial proceedings reveals that Babo had led a successful revolt on board, killed Cereno's friend Aranda, who was also the owner of the slave cargo, and forced the remaining whites to participate in a dumbshow of

Volume 19, Number 2   DOI 10.1215/10407391-2008-003

orderliness so as not to arouse the suspicions of Delano. We are told that Delano's obtuseness in fact saved his life, and there are clear indications that he has learned nothing of moral value from the experience.

Melville presents Delano as a genial racist and, through his extraordinary manipulation of narrative voice, forces the reader into uncomfortably close proximity to the American's undiscerning point of view. The proximity is uncomfortable because we are allowed neither to identify fully with Delano nor to extricate ourselves satisfactorily from his experience. In the third paragraph of the tale, Melville opens the narrative fissure he thenceforth forces us awkwardly to straddle: Captain Delano was a "person of a singularly undistrustful good nature," we are told, a man

> *not liable, except on extraordinary and repeated incentives, and hardly then, to indulge in personal alarms, any way involving the imputation of malign evil in man. Whether, in view of what humanity is capable, such a trait implies, along with a benevolent heart, more than ordinary quickness and accuracy of intellectual perception, may be left to the wise to determine. (673)*

We are invited here to take up a position of "wisdom," a position at some distance from the constellation of values—good nature, humanity, benevolence—that compromise Delano's ability to see what is right before his eyes. But if Melville invites us to exercise such wisdom, that does not mean that he provides the means to do so. In fact, Melville's tale ultimately suggests that the most profound question is not how Delano could be so stupid, but rather, how could he—and we—*not* be?

Can a historical event be indiscernible to the very actors involved in its unfolding? "The Haitian Revolution [. . .] entered history with the peculiar characteristic of being unthinkable even as it happened," writes Michel-Rolph Trouillot in *Silencing the Past: Power and the Production of History* (73). What does it mean for an event to be "unthinkable"? Trouillot is not of course denying that between 1791 and 1804, African and Creole slaves rose up en masse and, in a series of shifting alliances with various *gens de couleur* and some whites, went on to overthrow the plantation economy, force recognition of a general emancipation, repulse attempts by outside powers to retake the island, and ultimately take the reins of government and proclaim the independence of the first black state in the Western hemisphere. All this occurred, and no one denies it. Trouillot's point is, rather, that "the Haitian Revolution" was unthinkable because the *meaning* of these occurrences, taken as an ensemble, was illegible. Trouillot has the incomprehension of the white planters foremost in mind, though finally he extends the charge of failing to grasp the meaning of the event to non-Haitian observers in the Caribbean, North America, and Europe, as well as much of the subsequent historiographic tradition. The pervasiveness and extent of this problem of historical misprision is what I wish to explore in this essay; and indeed, we will see later in what sense even the revolutionaries were hard pressed to name the event. But for the white participants and observers especially, we could say that while things occurred, the event did not "take place." If these contemporaries of the Haitian revolution could not foresee its coming, could not discern it as it arrived, could not acknowledge its ongoing status, and could not process its summary meaning, it is because the idea of "considering the former slaves as the main actors in the chain of events" was not really plausible, according to Trouillot (104). The slaves were too obedient, too timid, too stupid, too incapable of organizing themselves.

Melville presents Delano's obtuseness as a function of his limited theory of human nature—an instinctive unwillingness to impute "malign evil" to humanity, a desire to exercise his "benevolent heart" (673). Delano sees himself, and Melville presents him, as a species of humanitarian, circa 1800. A problematic concept of humanity—human nature, even human rights—is ambiguously in play in the story of Haiti as well, and there, too, it is somehow part of the obscurity rather than the enlightenment. To say that the planters' assumptions about deficits in the slaves' abilities amount to a denial of their humanity, for example, is a simplification, as Trouillot shows. Say, rather, that the idea that there were "degrees of humanity" (76) proved a tremendously flexible instrument when it came to filling up the gap between the universalizing nature of the discourse of the "rights of man" and whatever adjustments of domination were perceived to be needed on the ground (see Dillon, "Secret"). It is not that the ideology of the "rights of man" has nothing to do with the origins, unfolding, or meaning of the Haitian revolution, in other words: any history of the complex series of events between 1791 and 1804 will indicate how often and in what varied contexts this concept was evoked.[1] But Trouillot argues that the discourses appealing to a universal humanity, discourses traditionally associated with the American and French revolutions, unveil themselves in the Haitian context in the mode of the missed encounter:

The Haitian Revolution was the ultimate test to the universalist pretensions of both the French and the American revolutions. And they both failed. In 1791, there is no public debate on the record, in France, in England, or in the United States on the right of black slaves to achieve self-determination, and the right to do so by way of armed resistance. *(88)*

To explore the problem of the indiscernible event, in Melville's tale and in the story of the Haitian revolution, I will have recourse to the ideas of Alain Badiou. Badiou's philosophy is challenging in many ways: based on an idiosyncratic manipulation of the axioms of set theory, Badiou's thought is highly abstract and forbiddingly systematic. Then, too, Badiou's political and ethical commitments are polemical and at times frankly disturbing, at least to this student. But as Badiou might say, genuine thinking is an adventure in fidelity, and one cannot judge what is of value in any text—Badiou's, Melville's, or the "text" of the Haitian revolution—if one does not linger therein, work with the terms that are given, risk an adherence to ideas and affective postures that are not immediately one's own.

At the heart of Badiou's theory lies his concept of the "event." Some of what this concept entails will be illuminated by what follows, but we can begin with what the event *is not* for Badiou. It is certainly not something that could be treated in a more or less positivistic manner, something that could, theoretically at least, be accounted for by an adequately exhaustive accounting of a context. Nor does Badiou's event resemble that of, say, trauma theory, an event that installs itself as an inaccessible wound. We began by asking how it could be possible for an event to be "unthinkable" to those involved in its unfolding. One of the most fertile theses of Badiou's philosophy of the event inverts this problem: "If there exists an event, *its belonging to the situation of its site is undecidable from the standpoint of the situation itself*" (*Being* 181). Rather than seeing the kind of historical blindness analyzed (and decried) by Trouillot as a shocking exception, Badiou suggests that the indiscernibility is an essential trait of any event worthy of the name, that is, as something understood as properly historical and not merely natural, not merely an occurrence subject to the regularities of nature and all that such regularities make possible by way of calculation, prediction, and ex post facto explanation.

The world is given to us, says Badiou; it appears as a presentation of multiplicity, a world of differences: "[I]n the situation (call it: the world) *there are differences*. One can even maintain that there is nothing else" (*Saint Paul* 98). But it is not this multiplicity of differences that interests Badiou, but rather the "nothing" that arrives, the event that can only be "nothing" from the point of view of the situation. Badiou's attitude toward the presentation of differences puts him squarely at odds with the valorization of difference in liberal ethics. As Peter Hallward comments, for Badiou, "[d]ifferences being simply *what there is*, the question of what 'ought to be' must concern only what is valid for all, at a level of legitimacy that is indifferent to differences. Differences *are*; the Same is what may *come to be* through the disciplined adherence to a universal truth" (Translator's xv). An ethics that does not consider truth is not worth the effort: "If truths exist, they are certainly indifferent to differences," Badiou writes in *Being and Event*. "A truth is solely constituted by rupturing with the order which supports it, never as an effect of that order" (xii). The valorization of difference is, in short, a mystification of liberalism:

> *That there are intertwined histories, different cultures and, more generally, differences already abundant in one and the "same" individual, that the world is multicolored, that one must let people live, eat, dress, imagine, love in whichever way they please, is not the issue, whatever certain disingenuous simpletons may want us to think. Such liberal truisms are cheap, and one would only like to see those who proclaim them not react so violently whenever confronted with the slightest serious attempt to dissent from their own puny liberal difference. (*Saint Paul 11*)

In a quite precise sense, this embrace of difference as a value in itself leads, in Badiou's opinion, to a culture of victimization. In his polemic against the ethical turn in philosophy, written in the 1990s, Badiou takes aim at "the presumption of a universal human Subject," a presumption that tends to reduce "ethical issues to matters of human rights and humanitarian actions" (*Ethics* 10). "Ethics thus defines man *as a victim*. It will be objected: 'No! You are forgetting the active subject, the one that intervenes against barbarism!' So let us be precise: man is *the being capable of recognizing himself as a victim*. It is this definition that we must proclaim unacceptable" (10–11). The humanitarian drama, we could say, encompasses both victimization and "intervention," since both positions place "man" always in the shadow of real or potential victimization. Against this reduction of human being to mere living substance, to "the haggard animal exposed on television screens" (13), Badiou insists that Man can be a "tissue of truths," not an individual but a "Subject": for in "each case, subjectivation is immortal, and makes Man. Beyond this there is only a biological species, a 'biped without feathers,' whose charms are not obvious" (12). A concept of the "human" is wrested from a hypocritical practice of "humanitarianism" here: in proposing that the human names a range of differences, that there are varieties of humanness (varieties that ultimately boil down to the basic dyad of victim and victimizer), this "humanitarianism" in fact betrays the "human," which is, for Badiou, a condition that is precisely the same for all—a "tissue of truths."

I will not criticize Badiou's contempt for human animality here (I have elsewhere: see Elmer). But as our brief glances at *Benito Cereno* and Trouillot on Haiti have shown, the indiscernible event and the problem of the human, and human rights, seem entangled in one another. Badiou is disquietingly harsh on this subject, but he is not alone: humanitarian values and concepts have increasingly become stumbling blocks for a wide range of contemporary critical thought. Badiou asks us: does the "human" or "Man," the human understood as endowed with "rights," name a regime of differences, or is it instead the object of some kind of universal address, a "truth" in Badiou's sense, necessarily indifferent to differences? Our contemporary moment cannot help but raise the question of the historicity and validity of the concept of human rights. On the one hand, the discourse of human rights has arguably never been more prevalent; on the other hand, the flagrant disregard for its most basic principles by those states and figureheads who profess to defend it is there for all to see. High-profile attempts to historicize the concept, like Lynn Hunt's *Inventing Human Rights: A History*, cannot help seeming incapable of telling us what we most need to know. For it is the *relation between* the historical emergence of the concept and its universal address that we need to understand. Badiou's thought is especially provocative on these questions, since his disdain for "humanitarianism" is matched by his exaltation of universal—immortal and infinite—truths and of the human subjects who sustain such truths through their militant fidelity. The hinge between an always saturated field of differences and the truth that necessarily supercedes such differences is what Badiou theorizes as the "event." This event is always subject to misprision, always in need of renewed interpretive intervention and creative nomination, and is the point of leverage in the struggle between a universalism of differences and that of truth.

Le Nom Français Lugubre Encore
Nos Contrées

When Trouillot writes that "the Haitian Revolution [. . .] entered history with the peculiar characteristic of being unthinkable even as it happened," part of what is at stake for him is the inherent ambiguity that obtains between "sociohistorical process" and the "narrative constructions about that process." These "two sides of historicity" (24) are not sequentially separable, but are, rather, always co-implicated: historical experience is always a mixture of process and narrative. Trouillot argues that "[h]istory, as social process, involves peoples in three distinct capacities: (1) as *agents*, or occupants of structural positions; (2) as *actors* in constant interface with a context; and (3) as *subjects*, that is, as voices aware of their vocality" (23). Let us call Trouillot's *agent* a slave in the French Caribbean, and his *actor*—a "bundle of capacities that are specific in time and space" (23)—a slave named Boukman who worked as a driver and a coachman (Dubois, *Avengers* 99). When that same Boukman leads a religious ceremony during which he incites his fellow slaves to take revenge against their white oppressors, urging them to "listen to the voice of liberty that speaks in the hearts of all of us" (100), we have what Trouillot would call a *subject*.

Trouillot's immediate example is not the Haitian revolution, however, but a strike:

> *[P]eoples are also the subjects of history the way workers are subjects of a strike: they define the very terms under which some situations can be described. [. . .] There is no way to describe a strike without making the subjective capacities of the workers a central part of the description. Stating their absence from the workplace is certainly not enough. We need to state that they collectively reached the decision to stay at home on what was supposed to be a regular working day. [. . .] Thus, beyond dealing with the workers as actors, a competent narrative of a strike needs to claim access to the workers as purposeful subjects aware of their own voices. [. . .] To put it most simply, a strike is a strike only if the workers think that they are striking. Their subjectivity is an integral part of the event and of any satisfactory description of the event. (23–24)*

At first sight, Trouillot's theory here is not about the indiscernibility of an event, but rather its opposite: certain events can *only* be said to take place

when they are self-consciously acknowledged to be doing so. The nomination of the event is a part of it. A gathering of workers outside the workplace
is not a strike unless the workers call it one: the event and its description
are necessarily tied to one another. But this requirement of nomination
also means that events can be undone, denied, misrecognized by the sheer
power of the misnomer: the strike, say, is just an illegal gathering. Or the
revolution is merely a rebellion, a revolt, a conspiracy of runaways, a few
agitators stirring up trouble.

It is this power of misnaming, this misrecognition, that Trouillot most immediately has in mind when he says that the Haitian revolution "was unthinkable even as it happened." He quotes a planter writing
just months before the first uprising: "The Negroes are very obedient and
always will be. We sleep with doors and windows wide open. Freedom for
Negroes is a chimera" (72). We see the power of magical thinking here, as
visible in the commitment to changelessness (the Negroes "always will be"
obedient) as in the mythical stamp—"a chimera"—with which the planter
hopes to obscure his own language's presentation of freedom: "freedom
for Negroes *is* . . . ." We see a battle being waged within language itself,
as it were, syntax and figure pressed into service to make sure that certain nominations do not appear. Historical blindness must be vigilantly
maintained, in other words, even if that means according it the kind of
reflective acknowledgment we see emerging in a letter from a plantation
manager written to his absentee employer just a month after the uprising
in Le Cap began in August 1791:

> *There is a motor that powers [the insurgent slaves] and that*
> *keeps powering them and that we cannot come to know. All*
> *experienced colons know that this class of men has neither the*
> *energy nor the combination of ideas necessary for the execution*
> *of this project, whose realization they nevertheless are marching*
> *toward with perseverance. (qtd. in Dubois,* Colony *109–10)*

The "knowledge" of the "experienced colons" is not called into question
here, not exposed as false knowledge. The manager does not consider
changing his views, he merely acknowledges the unfolding of a historical entelechy—a "motor" and a "project"—that is beyond his ken, and
definitively so: something "we cannot come to know."

There seems, then, to be both an acknowledgment of something
happening that cannot be known and a series of efforts to repress, through
misnaming, this knowledge. The central strategy, here, was what we might

call, in Trouillot's terminology, the restriction of the insurgents to the level of *actors*, rather than *subjects*, of the uprising. Slave rebellion was as a rule reduced to a narrative about individuals: the defiant, resistant, or "runaway emerges from this literature—which still has its disciples— as an animal driven by biological constraints, at best a pathological case" (Trouillot 83). This denial of collective agency was self-serving, of course, ultimately designed to protect the planters from a systemic view of their situation: "To acknowledge resistance as a mass phenomenon is to acknowledge the possibility that something is wrong with the system" (84). Even as the plantations burned around them, slaveowners circulated stories designed to blind them to the meaning of the unfolding events. These were stories about individual slaves:

> *What made the "horrors" of the insurrection even worse was the betrayal of especially trusted slaves such as drivers and domestics. One account lamented that it was the slaves "which had been most kindly treated by their masters" that were "the soul of the Insurrection." [. . .] It was a "heart-breaking discovery" to the planters, who would see nothing but despair in the future were it not for certain acts of "invincible fidelity" by certain slaves. Such loyal slaves had received their liberty in thanks, but—and this was crucial—this liberty was "the gift of their masters." Seeking to hold onto a world that was burning all around them, white masters sought relief in stories of fidelity that provided the consoling mirage that their world could once again be as it had been. (Dubois,* Avengers *112)*

Whether the story concerned betrayal or fidelity finally matters much less than that the insurrection is understood as a story of individual actors, and not subjects. Betrayal/fidelity names a structure within which individuals can change places, while keeping the groundlessness of the structure itself out of view. Betrayal/fidelity naturalizes, or humanizes, a structure we might as well call the master/slave dialectic. Susan Buck-Morss has argued that Hegel developed his idea in reaction to news from Haiti but erased all traces of such influence in abstracting the dialectic into a general principle of historical becoming. Hegel extracts an engine of historical eventfulness from the news from Haiti, as it were, but at the cost of losing sight of how this engine itself represents a willed simplification of a more complex reality, an attempt to make history a matter of individuals—actors, in Trouillot's sense—forever negotiating their positions in a dynamic of domination and subjugation, rather than the more aleatory process in which "master" and "slave" represent forms of repressive nomination against a background of a general freedom ("Freedom for Negroes *is* . . ."). This freedom is no less real for being strictly virtual. Buck-Morss asks at the close of her essay: "What if every time that the consciousness of individuals surpassed the confines of present constellations of power in perceiving the concrete meaning of freedom, *this* were valued as a moment, however transitory, of the realization of absolute spirit?" (865). To surpass the confines of present constellations of power presumably means for Buck-Morss the ability to see the limitations of the master/slave (betrayal/fidelity) dialectic, to see that freedom in its concreteness is what is subtracted, as it were, from the dialectical constellation. Like the planters, Hegel wants to individualize, and so naturalize, a historical process in which what Trouillot calls subjects are inescapably at work.

Trouillot had also touched on what I suggested was a virtual dimension of freedom in his example of the strike:

> *Workers work much more often than they strike, but the capacity to strike is never fully removed from the condition of workers. In other words, peoples are not always subjects constantly confronting history as some academics would wish, but the capacity upon which they act to become subjects is always part of their condition. This subjective capacity ensures confusion because it makes human beings doubly historical or, more properly, fully historical. It engages them simultaneously in the sociohistorical process and in narrative constructions about that process. (24)*

Being a subject of history, and not merely an actor, is something that one must "become" by realizing, literally, that the capacity to do this is always there, "never fully removed." Becoming a subject of history involves a decision, as it were, about an ever-present possibility, and it is a decision that "ensures confusion," since the process and the narrative about that process are in a necessary but out-of-phase relation to one another. And the decision here also concerns a dimension that remains orthogonal to business as usual: striking is not in a dialectical relation to working. A worker might, under certain conditions, decide to stop being a worker and start being a manager, but to invoke the capacity to strike is to activate a primal background negation of things as they are. It is to "subtract" a truth of freedom from the presented situation.

This last phrase is Badiouvian in nomenclature, and I need to pause now to suggest how much of what we have touched on already is filtered through Badiou's way of conceiving of the event. We have seen that Badiou sees the world as given to us as a field of differences and multiplicity (indeed, all entities or items presented in the world are themselves called "multiples" by Badiou, in keeping with his set-theoretical axiomatics). This world of differences is a world of presentation, a world that, it is important to recognize, is never chaotic: the "situation," as Badiou minimally defines it, is always subject to an operation of structuring, a "count-as-one." "One must not forget that every situation is structured. The multiple is retroactively legible therein as *anterior* to the one, insofar as the count-as-one is always a *result*" (*Being* 24). But this operation of structuring, the count-as-one, "cannot present itself; it can only operate" (25). Badiou is confronting the paradox that there cannot be a set of all sets here, a paradox whose exigency both incites—and inevitably undermines—the second structuring pass over every situation that Badiou argues always occurs. This second "count of the count," this (failed) attempt to secure the operation itself as included in what it structures, is what Badiou refers to, in avowed analogy to politics, as the *state* of the "situation." Building on certain theses of set theory, Badiou suggests that for every structured situation, defined in terms of *belonging*, there is a metastructuring moment, a "state of the situation," defined in terms of *inclusion*. It is in the ineliminable divergence between the situation and the state, however, that what Badiou—again borrowing from set theory—calls the "void" wanders about (Badiou's preferred metaphor is "errancy"), and this void underlies presentation itself. The state is always committed to foreclosing or denying the errancy of the void, usually by naturalizing all elements in presentation such that what belongs is also shown to be included, while everything else is expelled: "[T]he illegal and the unpresentable are precisely what [the state] expels" (208). For those who intervene in a decisive way as concerns the advent of an event, however, the same ambiguity becomes something that can be exploited.

Even with such a truncated account of Badiou's ideas, some important theses can be linked to the problems we have begun to examine with respect to the indiscernibility of the Haitian revolution. The first point is that the structure of retroactivity is fundamental. This is obvious with regard to the state and its metastructuring, via inclusion, of any and every situation: as "count of the count," the state subjects the world of presentation to an after-the-fact "re-presentation." But this retroaction is, it turns out, already inherent in the world of presentation itself: the fact that there is not chaos, that "every situation is structured," means that the world of differences with which we are always presented is already a result but one that must retroactively be understood to be an encounter between pure (inconsistent) multiplicity and the structuring effects of the count. This is important because what often looks like a problem only for a second-order activity—say, the historian writing up the Haitian revolution after the fact—is shown to be fundamental not only to representation, but also in the world of presentation itself. *Historical experience is itself always subject to the same retroaction as historiographical reflection*, a thesis that essentially confirms Trouillot's insistence on the "confusions" of humans' "doubly historical" existence as always simultaneously involved in sociohistorical process and narrative (retroactive) construction of that process.

The important question for Badiou, as concerns the political and ethical dimension of the event, is what strategies are brought to bear on this necessary confusion. Here is where we can return to the role of nomination. For Badiou, an essential element of an event is its own name, or the way in which it presents itself as "a *term* of the event that it is" (180). His example of the French Revolution is fortuitous, since as we will see in more detail in what follows, the French Revolution—or indeed more generally the French State, or what Dessalines calls *le nom Français*—plays a crucial and ambiguous role in the confusions about the ongoing event of the Haitian revolution:

> *Take the syntagm "the French Revolution." What should be understood by these words? One could certainly say that "the French Revolution" forms a one out of everything which makes up its site; that is, France between 1789 and, let's say, 1794. [. . .] The historian ends up including in the event "the French Revolution" everything delivered by the epoch as traces and facts. This approach, however—which is the inventory of all the elements of the site—may well lead to the one of the event being undone to the point of being no more than the forever infinite numbering of the gestures, things, and words that co-existed with it. The halting point for this dissemination is* the mode in which the Revolution is a central term of the Revolution itself; *that is, the manner in which the conscience of the times—and the retroactive intervention of our own—filters the entire site through the one of its eventual qualification. When, for example,*

> *Saint-Just declares in 1794 "the Revolution is frozen," he is certainly designating infinite signs of lassitude and general constraint, but he also adds to them that* one-mark *that is the Revolution itself, as this signifier of the event which, being qualifiable (the Revolution is "frozen"), proves that it is itself a term of the event that it is. (*Being *180)*

Badiou says that this "signifier of the event" "proves" itself to be "a term of the event that it is," but he also knows full well that no such proof is ever available—either for the "conscience of the times" or for "the retroactive intervention of our own" (and I have just indicated how these two are structurally alike). There is no "proof" about the signifier of the event because it is always subject to an interpretive decision. Recall:

> *If there exists an event,* its belonging to the situation of its site is undecidable from the standpoint of the situation itself. *That is, the signifier of the event [. . .] is necessarily supernumerary to the site. [. . .] [O]nly an* interpretative intervention *can declare that an event is presented in a situation; as the arrival in being of non-being, the arrival amidst the visible of the invisible. (181)*

Let us return to Trouillot's version of this idea: the strike. Trouillot suggested "a strike is a strike only if the workers think that they are striking. Their subjectivity is an integral part of the event and of any satisfactory description of the event" (23–24). We might say that a strike presents both the "inventory" of all the terms of its site—the workers walking off the job, their gathering at an indicated location, their notification of press and employers, their posture toward scabs, and so on—and the "supernumerary" signifier of the event, the nomination "strike." That this nomination is supernumerary is testified to by the fact that it can fail to be recognized; it is an "interpretative intervention" that can be disputed. Ronald Reagan did not recognize the air traffic controllers to be striking in 1980; their failure to work was, rather, *illegal,* and in general the state will deem as illegal any event that announces the "arrival in being of non-being, the arrival amidst the visible of the invisible." Although workers work more than they strike, as Trouillot said, their capacity to strike is always with them: this capacity to not work, I suggested earlier, is a kind of background condition to working, a virtual foundation to being (working) of non-being (not working), an incursion into the visible of the invisible ("What are you doing?" "Nothing." "You can't do nothing." "We are doing nothing and we call it striking"). "The act of nomination of the event," writes Badiou, "is what constitutes it, not as real—we will always posit that this multiple has occurred—but as susceptible to a decision concerning its belonging to the situation" (*Being* 203).

The Haitian revolution, by this reckoning, announces itself as an event properly speaking precisely *because* of its ongoing indiscernibility. It was "susceptible to a decision"—and perhaps it remains so, in the sense that its status as revolutionary event remains in dispute. I broke off my discussion of the revolution just when I made what may well have seemed a violent swerve from the planters of St. Domingue to Hegel, suggesting that they shared a strategy of individualizing actors in order not to see an event unfolding. The Haitian revolution is not an event for Hegel. Perhaps we will now be less surprised that if the Haitian revolution was unthinkable for the whites on the ground, it has proved no less so for the entire Western philosophical and historiographical tradition. Trouillot calls the planters' strategy of pathologizing individual rebellion a "caricature of methodological individualism. Would each single explanation be true, the sum of all of them would say little of the causes and effects of the repetition of such cases" (84). Something formally similar is at work in the technique of "banalization" deployed by a certain historical consciousness: this strategy aims to "empty a number of singular events of their revolutionary content so that the entire string of facts, gnawed from all sides, becomes trivialized" (96). Historical positivism—draining events by reducing them to mere facts—and methodological individualism are strategies shared by planters and historians alike, and they testify to the "unthinkability" of the revolution: "Official debates and publications of the times, including the long list of pamphlets on Saint-Domingue published in France from 1790 to 1804, reveal the incapacity of most contemporaries to understand the ongoing revolution on its own terms" (73).

But what precisely *are* the revolution's "own terms," after all? Badiou suggests that the "supernumerary signifier" is a "*term* of the event that it is" (180). Can we find such terms that are at once immanent and supernumerary in the Haitian revolution? Trouillot is disinclined to allow those terms to be the familiar ones of revolutionary universalism, of the discourse of the rights of man and general emancipation that we associate with the French Revolution. It has been assumed, from the earliest moments of the insurrection to the present day, that the radical ideas finding historical expression in France were themselves catalysts for the Haitian revolution. But the "assumption that the French connection is both sufficient and necessary to the Haitian Revolution [. . .] trivializes the slaves' independent sense of their right to freedom and the right to achieve this freedom by force of arms" (104). Recall Trouillot's summary judgment: "The Haitian Revolution was the ultimate test to the universalist pretensions of both the French and the American revolutions. And they both failed" (88).

But this way of grasping the problem seems to ignore the play of nomination and indiscernibility that we have been exploring. If it is true that the French revolution was neither "necessary nor sufficient" for the Haitian revolution, it is not therefore the case that it is irrelevant. Laurent Dubois, whose recent histories of the revolutionary "sequences" in the French Caribbean are as up to date as any, has demonstrated just how complex and contradictory action and ideology were throughout this period. While it seems clear that certain rumors about a coming emancipation were eagerly seized upon in the build up to the revolt in 1791, hopes were at first pinned on the king rather than any Republican radicalism, and in any case such rumors were hardly unprecedented in the region, for obvious reasons. The insurgents did avail themselves of emancipationist rhetoric, as had the free *gens de couleur* in their own battle for political rights with the white planter class: "Like revolutionaries in France, black insurgents expressed themselves by speaking and acting—uninvited—in the name of the French nation, and in so doing they brought about the declarations that officially made them part of that nation" (*Colony* 89). But what needs to be kept clearly in view here is the way in which nomination both precedes and results from ongoing action, such that the paradoxes of retroaction are in play throughout. The insurgency is both supported by and productive of a series of contested nominations. What this means is that the event of the revolution was no more certain as something that existed for the insurgents themselves than it was for their opponents. It was, rather, what Badiou might call a "wager" (*Being* 201). The revolutionary sequence constitutes a "situation," a condition of the pure presentation of differences from within which the existence of an event is necessarily an undecidable phenomenon. For that reason, an essential aspect of its action was the interpretive intervention involved in naming the event, a nomination that, for reasons Badiou exposes, was simultaneously pro- and retroactive. Dubois describes this situation this way:

> *Whether outsiders encouraged the enslaved to revolt, the insurrection took a course unimagined and unexpected, even for the*

insurgents themselves. The initial demands of the rebels were not for full emancipation: according to one captured slave's testimony, at a meeting called to organize the revolt "a statement was read by an unknown mulatto or quadroon to the effect that the King and the National Assembly in France had decreed three free days a week for every slave, as well as the abolition of the whip as a form of punishment." Insurgents repeated demands for "three days" during the early months of the revolt. Only through the insurrection was the goal of complete emancipation imagined and then solidified as a project. *(Colony 109, emphasis added)*

None of the key players in this complex drama went into it with general emancipation as a stated project—not the initial insurgents, not the Jacobin commissioner Sonthonax, who would eventually proclaim it under pressure of events, not Louverture, who made his way toward undisputed command of the colony by way of fighting for the Spanish, then for the French, then against the French. But this does not mean that emancipation was not integral to the unfolding of the event. Emancipation was less the guiding political project, goal, or telos, we might say, than it was a kind of enabling condition. That the slaves were free, in other words, in some concrete though brutally denied sense, is the necessary background condition of the actions undertaken in the name of those values, pronouncements, and theses—universal human rights, the French Republic, the French monarchy—that were, at different times and to different ends, ready to hand. Just because the revolution did not unfold as the realization of a stated project of legal and complete emancipation for the slaves, it does not follow that such emancipation is nothing more than merely an item in the "inventory" to be presented in any account of the Haitian revolution. What must be understood is that the event itself, and the fidelity to its status as ongoing, is superior to the differences that take shape in these and such ways. That is, we need to see the freedom that subtends the historical intervention in the first place as named by, but also in excess of, something called general emancipation, such that it is still in play when emancipation is not yet "projected."

It is extraordinarily tempting to oversimplify the meaning of the Haitian revolutionary sequence. The simplifications were widely at work already between 1791 and 1804, and they continued throughout the following decades to divide historical propagandists on either side of the fence.[2] Abolitionist agitators later in the nineteenth century tended to idealize the actions and personalities of the central actors, a strategy still in favor among nationalist historians in Haiti (Trouillot 105). Reactionary forces, on the other hand, hewed close to the strategy of denial we have already examined: the new Haitian state was not officially recognized by the United States until 1862, for example, and in general the revolution, as most modern commentators point out, has been dismissed as mere rebellion, pointless carnage, a relatively isolated eruption marked by the seemingly unprincipled switching of allegiances among many key leaders and factions, or occasionally a genuinely revolutionary moment that quickly subsided into strong-man despotism under Louverture, Christophe, and others. The revolution begins to look from this vantage like merely another rebellion collapsing back on itself. In this way, too, the "revolution that was unthinkable becomes a non-event" (98): as Trouillot and others have pointed out, even Eric Hobsbawm's *Age of Revolutions, 1789–1843* barely mentions Haiti.

How can we avoid this simplification? We can start by recognizing that if differences are just what there is, as Badiou says, there is no possibility of somehow wishing them away: in the Haitian situation these differences would encompass the system of racial designations, varieties of freedom and citizenship status, the multiple and constantly shifting modalities by which one could assert a faithfulness to land, language, monarch, republic, or people. The militant adherent of the truths that suspend such differences can only make his way to such truths on the back, as it were, of the differences that are there. In his book on Saint Paul, Badiou suggests that Paul evidenced a

> *highly characteristic militant tonality, combining the appropriation of particularities with the immutability of principles, the empirical existence of differences with their essential nonexistence, according to a succession of problems requiring resolution, rather than through an amorphous synthesis. (99)*

To read of Louverture's insistently pragmatic jockeying through the years of warfare and command is to see something similar at work. In October 1800, Toussaint "militarized plantation labor": "[T]he status of the plantation laborer—a status based on a past of enslavement on the very plantations where they were now being ordered to stay—was rendered immutable and permanent. All efforts to escape this past and to create a different future—other than for service in Louverture's army—were criminalized." This is a shocking turn of events, and Dubois writes with good reason that "Louverture had turned himself into a dictator" (*Avengers* 239). But to see this development as simply a turn of the screw in an ongoing, and unchanging, dialectic of domination and subjugation is to miss the fact that, for those on the ground, another dimension was still in play. By 1800, everything in the situation, including the new militarization of the plantation labor system, was, as Badiou would say, "filtered through [the] eventual name" of revolutionary emancipation. The workers in Haiti apparently thought this recognition by the revolution of an always latent, and indeed, invisible freedom, superseded the "empirical existence of differences" under which they continued to groan: "[T]hose French who confused Louverture's regime with slavery were also in for a rude awakening. Despite the many limits he had placed on freedom, the ex-slaves clearly saw the difference between the present and the past. And they were willing to lay down their lives rather than go back" (250).

The continuing and ineradicable grip of the interplay between nomination and the situation of empirical differences is evident in the 1804 constitution to the newly proclaimed independent state of Haiti. Louverture's 1801 constitution had proclaimed general emancipation but had also avoided proclaiming full political sovereignty. Article 3 read: "There can be no slaves in the territory; servitude is forever abolished. Here, all men are born, live, and die, free and French" (qtd. in Fischer 229). But after Louverture's capture and the ferociously brutal battles against Leclerc and Rochambeau, Dessalines's declaration of independence in January 1804 was aimed specifically at the French: "Everything revives memories of the cruelties of these barbarous people: our laws, our habits, our towns, everything still carries the stamp of the French" (qtd. in Dubois, *Avengers* 298). The very name of the island must be changed, replaced by that reputed to have been used by the indigenous Taino inhabitants. "Le nom français lugubre encore nos contrées": The French name still haunts our lands (Dubois, *Avengers* 298; see also Fischer 201–2). As Dubois, Fischer, and others have pointed out, *lugubrer* is a neologism that endows the adjective *lugubre*, meaning gloomy or dismal, with the active force of a verb—to make lugubrious, perhaps. Dubois translates *lugubrer* as "haunt" above, and Fischer suggests "grieves." Perhaps "shadows" could work as well: the French name still shadows our lands. But from our vantage what is so compelling about this poetic invention is its testimony of a struggle of nomination. The work of naming the event must pass through the names and the differences that are presented to us. The event is not reducible to those names, but rather, if you are lucky, it leaves behind traces of its impact, its power to bend and force, as *lugubre* is stretched to make *lugubrer*. What applies to words and names also applies to the other inherited identities presented time out of mind by the situation of Haiti. Fischer writes some compelling pages about Articles 12 through 14 of the new constitution. Article 12 makes it illegal for any white person "of whatever nationality" to acquire property or "set foot on this territory in the role of master or proprietor" (qtd. in Fischer 232). Article 13 exempts naturalized white women from the previous stipulation, as well as their present or future children, and all Germans and Poles naturalized by the government. Article 14 reads: "All distinctions of color will by necessity disappear among the children of one and the same family, where the Head of State is the father; Haitians will henceforth be known by the generic denomination of blacks" (232). As Fischer observes, "Calling all Haitians, regardless of skin color, black [. . .] both asserts egalitarian and universalist intuitions and puts them to a test by using a previously subordinated term of the opposition as the universal term" (233). I would see this less as a "test," however, than a testimony of the struggle between universality and the givenness of identities and difference, a struggle playing out in terms of nomination, between the idea of "generic denomination" and the terms *black* and *white*. The difficulty of seeing anything around the edges of these identities, in their inversions and reversals, their "blacks and whites," is much in evidence here and accounts, perhaps, for why Dessalines remains so *lugubre* even at the moment of emancipation.

Babo's Razor

At the end of Herman Melville's *Benito Cereno*, there is a well-known conversation between Don Benito, the Spanish captain of the *San Dominick*, and Amasa Delano, who had somehow managed, at the last minute, to realize what had transpired on the ship, what was even then transpiring, and to retake Cereno's ship from the rebellious slaves that had seized control. "You generalize, Don Benito; and mournfully enough," begins Delano.

> "But the past is passed; why moralize upon it? Forget it. See, yon bright sun has forgotten it all, and the blue sea, and the blue sky; these have turned over new leaves."

> "Because they have no memory," he dejectedly replied; "because they are not human." (754)

The human and the natural are antithetical, in Cereno's view. Delano wishes to assert the continuity between natural and human existence, on the other hand; he invokes patterns of change as recurrence: turning over new leaves, suns going up and down. The implication is that whatever revolutions may have occurred in the human world, they are versions of these natural cycles. Cereno, by contrast, sees something in the human condition that is not susceptible to natural explanation or the assuagement of the "human-like healing" of the trade winds fanning the two captains as they speak. "'You are saved,' cried Captain Delano, more and more astonished and pained; 'you are saved; what has cast such a shadow upon you?' 'The negro'" (754). Does "the negro" mean Babo? Does it mean all negroes? Cereno's enigmatic remark recalls the torque and tension between universal and particular we saw at work in the nominations of the Haitian revolution: indeed, as Dessalines finds himself beneath the *lugubre* French name, so Cereno is shadowed by the name of "the negro."

The relation between nomination and the indiscernible event takes a different form in *Benito Cereno* than in the history we have just reviewed, a form at once simpler and yet more mysterious. Melville based his story, as scholars have long known, on the historical Amasa Delano's *A Narrative of Voyages and Travels in the Northern and Southern Hemispheres* (1817). He follows Delano's text quite closely in many details: the names Cereno, Babo, and Atufal, for example, are all derived from the 1817 text. Newton Arvin suggested long ago that Melville was "too tired to rewrite at all, and except for a few trifling details, he leaves it all as he found it, in the drearily prosaic prose of a judicial deposition" (239). Two of the details that Arvin presumably finds "trifling" are Melville's renaming of the ship from the *Tryal* to the *San Dominick* and his moving the action of the story back a few years, from 1805 to 1799. Eric Sundquist has made the most elaborate argument that these changes signal Melville's intention to encrypt the story of the Haitian revolution in his own story of slave revolt and misprision. In 1799, the revolution was an ongoing affair, after all, and the colony was still called Saint-Domingue; by 1805, the nation of Haiti had been proclaimed. Given that he does not see this name change as significant, it is perhaps not surprising that Arvin does not see the action of the story as especially important either: "It is certainly very credible that a shipload of African slaves should break out in mutiny, and massacre most of the white officers and crew" (240)—credible, but hardly anything to write home about. More surprising is that C. L. R. James also failed to comment on Melville's renaming of the ship. Despite having written the definitive history of the Haitian revolution for his time, *The Black Jacobins: Toussaint l'Ouverture and the San Domingo Revolution* (1936), and despite describing Babo in terms he might have applied to Toussaint himself—"a man of unbending will, a natural leader, an organizer of large schemes but a master of detail" (*Renegades* 112)—James does not see Melville's tale as allegorizing the Haitian story. What is more, the story disappoints James as it had Arvin, because it is in the end mere "propaganda," a mere retelling of a very old and finally unremarkable story of an uprising: "The Negro slaves and their leaders are shown to be human," James concedes. But this mere humanity is oddly what makes the story ultimately insignificant: "[F]rom Spartacus to Zapata, history tells us ten thousand such stories. Melville had ceased to be creative" (112).

If Melville's most significant act of nomination in his story is to rename the ship the *San Dominick*, the significance of such an allusion seems as hard to discern as the meaning of the revolution itself. Such a naming is a kind of gamble, a wager, in Badiou's sense, and in this way also an announcement of fidelity. Melville gathers these themes—the willfulness of naming, its status as a gesture tokening fidelity, its submission to a situation that makes it difficult to draw distinctions—in his initial description of the ship itself:

> *Rudely painted or chalked, as in a sailor freak, along the forward side of a sort of pedestal below the canvas, was the sentence, "Seguid veustro jefe" (follow your leader); while upon the tarnished head-boards, near by, appeared, in stately capitals, once gilt, the ship's name, "SAN DOMINICK," each letter streakingly corroded with tricklings of copper-spike rust; while, like mourning weeds, dark festoons of sea-grass slimily swept to and fro over the name, with every hearse-like roll of the hull. (676)*

The name emerges from and subsides into the ocean, intermittently obscured by the sea grass that, perhaps prematurely, mourns its passing. Both the rebelling slaves and Melville indulge in "sailor freaks": acts of nomination and fidelity that simultaneously put the meaning, and even discernibility, of those acts radically in question. What does it mean to "follow your leader" in this story, after all? Who follows whom? If Melville invokes the name of Haiti in his story, then, he does so with the self-conscious understanding that such an invocation is a radical point of ambiguity, hard to spot, hard to interpret, even if spotted. Recall an earlier statement of Badiou's: "The act of nomination of the event is what constitutes it, not as real [. . .] but as susceptible to a decision concerning its belonging to a situation" (*Being* 203). At stake in the event called *Benito Cereno*, then, is its solicitation of a decision about whether Haiti belongs to it, and beyond that, about what status interpretation itself has with regard to the historicity of the event.

      Let us return to the conversation between Cereno and Delano with which we began this section. Delano clearly announces there his membership in the party of "nature." And indeed, Delano attempts to reduce everything, from the behavior of the slaves on board to the puzzling narrative of the ship's trouble at sea, to the terms of what he calls "naked nature" (Melville 704). He likens Babo's expression to that of a "shepherd's dog" (678), and indeed, Delano "took to Negroes [. . .] just as other men to Newfoundland dogs" (716). But Delano's naturalizing strategy does not require that humans be canine; an equally effective strategy stresses their nobility. It is this vision of human nature that Babo plays upon in the drama of Atufal. Atufal is made to appear before Cereno, in chains, in order to stage his refusal to beg pardon: "This is some mulish mutineer, thought Captain Delano, surveying, not without a mixture of admiration, the colossal form of the negro" (691). Delano's admiration here is crucial: he agrees with Cereno that one "could not scourge such a form" (691) and exclaims that "he has a royal spirit in him, this fellow" (692). Atufal represents a fantasy of innate dignity that is at once "docile" (692) and unsubdued. Delano thinks he is looking at human nature, a human nature that stays the same despite the revolutions in fortune that make some men masters and some slaves, some capable of granting pardon and others capable of refusing to beg for it. So blinded is Delano by this vision of a natural order as expressive of regular revolutions that he does not pause to think that, according to what Cereno tells him, this scene between the "royal" slave and the fainting captain has occurred 720 times! "'At my command every two hours he stands before me.' 'And how long has this been?' 'Some sixty days'" (691). Delano does not apparently need to reflect on the details of this drama of regularity and repetition: all he knows is that Atufal and Cereno, and all they convey in moral terms, are subject to a regime of regularity. Atufal is, in fact, a "time-piece" (727), a symbol of natural calculability.

      Why should Delano's commitment to "nature" be implicated in his blindness toward the event transpiring aboard the *San Dominick*? In Meditation 16 of *Being and Event*, Badiou argues that Nature is, as Delano in fact believes, the place of normalcy: it is, in fact, the "omnipresence of normality" (174). In Badiou's set-theoretical terms, a "normal" multiple is one that both belongs and is included: there is no divergence between presentation and representation, the situation and state of the situation, belonging and inclusion, in Nature. But precisely because of its "omnipresent normality," Nature has no "memory," as Cereno said; it is the site of "oblivion," in Badiou's words: "Nature, structural stability, equilibrium of presentation and representation, is rather that from which being-there weaves the greatest oblivion. Compact excess of presence and the count, nature buries inconsistency and turns away from the void. Nature is too global, too normal, to open up to the eventual convocation of its being" (177). In Melville's tale, Delano's myopia "buries inconsistency," seems an engine of this "oblivion": the American cannot see in terms other than those of "structural stability," a stability he extends to human affairs with their regular cycles.

But of course Delano is not the representative of Nature in itself, as Badiou describes it. He is, rather, a representative of the state, engaged in the kind of naturalizing—normalizing—behavior we have already encountered in the planters' tendency to reduce rebellion to a matter of individuals, rather than subjects. In Meditation 16, Badiou observes that there is a fundamental asymmetry between Nature and History when it comes to the process of normalization: "Nature is absolute, historicity relative," he writes. Historicity is a matter of "singularities," multiples that belong to the situation but are not included in the latter: "[T]he form-multiple of historicity is what lies entirely within the instability of the singular; it is that upon which the state's metastructure has no hold. It is a point of subtraction from the state's re-securing of the count" (174). The asymmetry between History and Nature concerns the latter's ability to normalize singularities: this is, indeed, what is at work in the operations of Delano's "good nature," as well as the entire legal postscript, another way in which Melville draws our attention to the ceaseless work of "re-securing [. . .] the count." From Delano's point of view, we might conclude, such a "re-securing" has occurred: hence his confidence in the healing humanlike regularities of the natural world. And it is true, Badiou insists, that singularities *can* be thus normalized. That which initially appears as presented but not represented can become represented, and thus normalized: "[A]ny evental site can, in the end, undergo a state normalization." The reverse, however, is not true: "[H]istory can be naturalized, but the natural cannot be historicized" (176).

The final conversation between Delano and Cereno, however, indicates that Melville does not think such a normalization of the singular, such a naturalization of history, has in fact occurred. The sun and sky "have no memory," insists Cereno. How does Melville make us see both the work of normalization and the "subtraction" of historicity that exposes that normalization as incomplete? It is here, once again, just where nature and historicity sheer off from one another, that the event, in all its indiscernible force, comes into play. For Badiou, if a situation is to be termed historical, it must contain at least one "evental site," that is, at least one multiple "that belongs to the situation, whilst what belongs to it in turn does not" (175). Peter Hallward has described the "evental site" in terms suggestive of Melville's text: "An evental site [. . .] is certainly in a situation, but it belongs to it as something uncertain, something whose own contents remain indiscernible and mysterious, if not sinister and threatening" (120). The *San Dominick*, in Melville's tale, is just such a site: erring and adrift, it is at once clearly something belonging to the whole situation, but also something that from the start is "sinister and threatening," charged with contents—are those monks in black cowls? No, they're slaves—that are, and indeed remain, "indiscernible and mysterious." The appearance of such evental sites within a situation is a great danger for the forces of normalization, for what is thereby exposed is the void itself, as that from which the world of presentation emerges: the "evental site" is, as Badiou expresses it, "on the edge of the void" (175). While for Delano, it is the *San Dominick* that is thus sinister and threatening, Melville's life-long meditation on the social and historical forces crystallized in the ship at sea allows him finally to see *every* ship as such an evental site, on the edge of the oceanic void, always potentially erring and drifting with that void, never fully able, from the vantage of an observer of the situation, to disclose its contents:

> *Always upon first boarding a large and populous ship at sea, especially a foreign one, with a nondescript crew such as Lascars or Manilla men, the impression varies in a peculiar way from that produced by first entering a strange house with strange inmates in a strange land. Both house and ship, the one by its walls and blinds, the other by its high bulwarks like ramparts, hoard from view their interiors till the last moment; but in the case of the ship there is this addition; that the living spectacle it contains, up on its sudden and complete disclosures, has, in contrast with the*

blank ocean which zones it, something of the effect of enchant-
ment. The ship seems unreal; these strange costumes, gestures,
and faces, but a shadowy tableau just emerged from the deep,
which directly must give back what it gave. (677)

Melville offers us the oceangoing ship as structurally a site of instability, emerging from and subsiding into the "blank [. . .] zones" of the
ocean, a site at once of heightened presentative intensity—an "effect of
enchantment"—and at the same time ineradicably opaque, "nondescript."
Melville describes the ship as an evental site within the global situation,
a place where historicity is at stake, where events may happen because
they are indiscernible as such.

But if this "enchantment" is structural, as it were, if it is not
only the *San Dominick* but any ship that induces the kind of myopia so bril-
liantly conveyed by Melville in his depiction of Delano, how are we to judge
that myopia in the final analysis? As we have seen, Melville seems to invite
us to take up a position of "wisdom" vis-à-vis Delano's faulty "quickness of
perception," but the drift of all we have said thus far is that such a vantage
is not to be had. The temptation to assume such a position is strong—which
is why Melville draws us toward it so early in the tale. The temptation is
of a kind of historical judgment, an interpretative distancing (as opposed
to an active intervention) that comes from the conviction that the context
has been effectively produced, the "inventory" of the situation assembled
in enough detail to admit of a correct placement of the meaning of the
event. We have seen a number of instances of people succumbing to this
temptation: Delano himself does so when he imagines that he understands
the meaning of the scene with Atufal, that he stands outside a dynamic
of bondage and freedom that even at that moment suspends him on its
razor's edge. Delano's own seduction by the master/slave dialectic, in the
scene with Atufal, arises from his idea that the historical can be thought
in terms of totalization. One of Badiou's strongest claims, it seems to me,
is that such a dream must be forsworn:

There are in the situation evental sites, but there is no evental
situation. We can think the historicity *of certain multiples,*
but we cannot think a History. *The practical—political—con-*
sequences of this conception are considerable, because they set
out a differential topology of action. The idea of an overturning
whose origin would be a state of a totality is imaginary. Every
radical transformational action originates in a point. *[. . .] It*

> *is solely in the point of history, the representational precarious-*
> *ness of evental sites, that it will be revealed, via the chance of a*
> *supplement, that being-multiple inconsists. (176–77)*

The allure of a revolutionary overturning, an upending of the status quo that starts again and in so starting reaffirms the totality of "*a* History," is as powerful for Delano looking at Atufal as it is to Dessalines struggling with "le nom Français." Against such a unitary, if ever-changing, History, Badiou sets a "historicity" that gathers us in its uncomfortable embrace by forcing us to decide, to interpret with no guarantee, whether the event has announced the arrival of the invisible in the midst of the visible. This commitment to what Badiou calls the "point of history" in its essential "representational precariousness" is what I take to be Melville's challenge in *Benito Cereno.* If he offers his tale as a gesture of fidelity to the Haitian revolution, it is in order to preserve the unfinishedness of it, its essential ambiguity, its solicitation of our own interpretive decision regarding its name. The inscrutableness of his tale, its ever-present liability to be misconstrued, is both its message and its method. We glimpsed before a virtual realm of freedom that exceeds, as it were, the regularities of work and order, on the one hand, and revolt and destruction, on the other. We might say, following Badiou, that this virtual freedom "inconsists." When Babo raises his razor over the lathered neck of Cereno, the "representational precariousness" of Melville's "evental site" reaches genuine vertigo. We may wish to fault Delano here again, but he is not blind: he sees both solicitude and menace, alternately, and who could do otherwise in any other situation? The servant's raised blade, in any situation governed by domination and subjection, will always open onto this same radical ambiguity. As Sundquist astutely remarks, Babo's "play of the barber" "both *is* and *is not*" (160); it announces the overflow of the real by the virtual. Melville asks us less to decide whether this point of history, this razor's edge, should, or will, caress or cut. Rather, he asks us to see that having to make such an interpretive judgment in the first place, and to do so with no guarantees, is how we remain faithful to the historicity of the event.

Many thanks to Lloyd Pratt, for the initial invitation to think about this topic and for his helpful feedback along the way, and to Josh Kates, for traveling much of this road with me.

JONATHAN ELMER teaches at Indiana University. He has published on Poe, Wright, Jefferson, Luhmann, and Lebowski, among others. His new book, *On Lingering and Being Last: Race and Sovereignty in the New World*, is forthcoming with Fordham University Press in 2008.

Notes   1   See Blackburn; Dubois, *Avengers*   2   See Blackburn; Fischer;
                   and *A Colony*; Fischer; Gaspar and   Sundquist; Trouillot.
                   Geggus.

Works Cited   Arvin, Newton. *Herman Melville*. Westport: Greenwood, 1950.

Badiou, Alain. *Being and Event*. 1988. Trans. Oliver Feltham. London: Continuum, 2005.

——————. *Ethics: An Essay on the Understanding of Evil*. Trans. Peter Hallward. London: Verso, 2002.

——————. *Saint Paul: The Foundation of Universalism*. Trans. Ray Brassier. Stanford: Stanford UP, 2003.

Blackburn, Robin. "Haiti, Slavery, and the Age of the Democratic Revolution." *William and Mary Quarterly* 63 (2006): 643–74.

Buck-Morss, Susan. "Hegel and Haiti." *Critical Inquiry* 26.4 (2000): 821–65.

Delano, Amasa. *A Narrative of Voyages and Travels in the Northern and Southern Hemispheres: Comprising Three Voyages Round the World; Together with a Voyage of Survey and Discovery in the Pacific Ocean and Oriental Islands*. 1817. New York: Praeger, 1970.

Dillon, Elizabeth Maddock. "Caribbean Revolution and Print Publics: Leonora Sansay and 'The Secret History of the Haitian Revolution.'" *Liberty! Égalité! ¡Independencia!: Print Culture, Enlightenment, and Revolution in the Americas, 1776–1838*. Ed. David S. Shields. Worcester: American Antiquarian Society, 2006. 133–53.

——————. "The Secret History of the Early American Novel: Leonora Sansay and Revolution in Saint Domingue." *The Early American Novel*. Ed. Leonard Tennenhouse. Spec. issue of *NOVEL: A Forum on Fiction* 40.1/2 (2006): 77–103.

Dubois, Laurent. *Avengers of the New World: The Story of the Haitian Revolution*. Cambridge: Harvard UP, 2004.

——————. *A Colony of Citizens: Revolution and Slave Emancipation in the French Caribbean, 1787–1804*. Chapel Hill: U of North Carolina P, 2004.

Elmer, Jonathan. "Torture and Hyperbole." *Law, Culture, and the Humanities* 3 (2007): 18–34.

Fischer, Sybille. *Modernity Disavowed: Haiti and the Cultures of Slavery in the Age of Revolution*. Durham: Duke UP, 2004.

Gaspar, David Barry, and David Patrick Geggus, eds. *A Turbulent Time: The French Revolution and the Greater Caribbean*. Bloomington: Indiana UP, 1997.

Hallward, Peter. *Badiou: A Subject to Truth*. Minneapolis: U of Minnesota P, 2003.

——————. Translator's Introduction. Badiou, *Ethics* vii–xxxv.

Hunt, Lynn. *Inventing Human Rights: A History*. New York: Norton, 2007.

James, C. L. R. *The Black Jacobins: Toussaint l'Ouverture and the San Domingo Revolution*. 2nd ed. New York: Vintage, 1989.

—————. *Renegades, Mariners, and Castaways: The Story of Herman Melville and the World We Live In*. Hanover: UP of New England, 2001.

Melville, Herman. *Benito Cereno*. 1855. In *The Piazza Tales*. New York: Library of America, 1984.

Sundquist, Eric J. *To Wake the Nations: Race in the Making of American Literature*. Cambridge: Harvard UP, 1993.

Trouillot, Michel-Rolph. *Silencing the Past: Power and the Production of History*. Boston: Beacon, 1995.

ANDREW AISENBERG

Bourdieu, Ambiguity, and the Significance of Events

Historians and Events

*T*he "event" constitutes one of the principal poles of historical analysis; "structure" is another. Events bring to mind the transformative capacity of individual agency, creativity, and contention in the making of social life, usually through a privileging of the spheres of politics and culture. Structural analysis attends to the importance of anonymous, impersonal trends as different as climate, wages, prices, and capitalist relations of production (including class) for determining the contours of social life. Historians often oppose event and structure as categories that engender contrasting portrayals or representations of social life. When historians ask whether a focus on the "event" will help us to understand human social experience in the past, they do so by gauging the relative explanatory merits (or inadequacy) of "structure," and vice versa. But some historians have refused this opposition. In *The Making of the English Working Class*, E. P. Thompson impressed upon historians the need to consider how workers made sense of the relations of production "into which they are born" (9). He pursued this task by paying attention to artisanal culture and the transformative events that comprised working-class mobilization and

Volume 19, Number 2   DOI 10.1215/10407391-2008-004

protest during the 1830s and 1840s. In his recent reflections on the relationship between history and theory, William Sewell attempts to surpass what he regards as the unproductive antimony of event and structure. As an alternative, he argues that the disarticulation of the complex of structures that define any specific historical moment opens up a space for the transformative effect of events and that such events in turn rearticulate the relationships among those structures.

My interest here is neither to resolve the ongoing debate about the adequacy of a focus on either events or structures for capturing social experience in the past, nor to evaluate recent efforts aimed at surpassing their opposition. Rather, I would like to address the humanistic assumptions that are shared by these approaches and that ground their purported opposition as well as the efforts of historians to think beyond their differences. For whether one chooses to study events as a way of demonstrating the centrality of human agency and creativity in social life or one aims at revealing the anonymous forces that determine capitalist relations of production (to name but one example of structure), the fact remains that both approaches assume the existence of qualities and capacities common to all human beings in the past—and the present. Even as sophisticated an intervention as Sewell's attempt to transcend the accepted event/structure opposition involves a commitment to a pluralistic vision of human society that accommodates conflict and differences of power within a larger field of common human capacities. Thus, Sewell states:

> *I would argue that a capacity for agency—for desiring, for forming intentions, and for acting creatively—is inherent in all humans. But I would also argue that humans are born with only a highly generalized capacity for agency [. . .]. The specific forms that agency will take consequently vary enormously and are culturally and historically determined. But a capacity for agency is as much a given for humans as the capacity for respiration. (144)*

The point here is not to criticize scholars who bring specific political interests and values to the task of historical writing. Rather, Sewell aims at identifying a more complex process: how legitimate historical evidence, generalizable categories of historical analysis (event, structure, or a specific combination of the two), and the humanistic assumptions guiding historians are mutually constituted. Beautifully crafted narrative renders palpable the heroic struggles of individuals and their capacity to shape their world, but its authority depends in part on the writer's (and readers') commitment to the sheer materiality of happenings or occurrences as a site for the expression of individual agency or creativity. Likewise, careful archival research and quantitative analysis bring to light the deep, anonymous yet inexorable influence of capitalist structures in the transformation of social life, but a recognition of the salience of these structures in the everyday lives of workers presupposes some kind of prior acknowledgment of the pervasive, even inevitable, role of industrial production in modernity.

Recognizing the mutual constitution of categories of historical analysis and humanistic assumptions about the defining characteristics of society invites different, and more difficult, questions than those commonly addressed in discussions involving the adequacy of a focus on events or structures. Such questions include: Do the specific formulations of supposedly general categories like event and structure reduce the complexity of social experience? How do these categories operate normatively so as to remove certain kinds of evidence from the historian's purview and limit what can be accepted as legitimate social experience? By accepting at face value understandings of conventional definitions of event and structure as generally applicable, do historians run the risk of missing the opportunity for a critical inquiry into the humanistic assumptions that inform (and are perpetuated by) those categories?

I want to follow the lines of critical inquiry suggested by these questions through a focus on Pierre Bourdieu and the central theoretical innovation of his work: habitus.[1] The choice is not an obvious one. Bourdieu was not a historian, but a sociologist with a strong ethnographic bent. His formulation of habitus is generally taken to be an important antifoundationalist contribution to structuralist approaches to the study of social organization. Central to his formulation of habitus is a critical engagement with the tendency of scholars to accept the parameters for the study of society largely in terms of a choice between subjectivist and objectivist perspectives. The widespread acceptance of the theoretical innovation of habitus has not precluded a good amount of scholarly controversy about its import.[2] There is a sense that Bourdieu's formulation of habitus is ambiguous, an ambiguity, moreover, that Bourdieu refused to dispel.

What if we refused to take this ambiguity as evidence of the limitations of the coherence of habitus and instead recognized in it the originality of Bourdieu's critique of the values of subjectivism and objectivism that are all too often assumed to be foundational, obvious, or inevitable?

Such an approach, among other things, would provide a potentially productive link between Bourdieu's work and the ongoing historical debate about event and structure. Not only do questions about the status of subjectivism and objectivism that inform Bourdieu's thinking about habitus also animate the debate about event and structure. More important (and what has generally been underappreciated by scholars), Bourdieu posed these questions and pursued answers to them in light of, and in direct relationship to, what historians regard as one of the defining events of the twentieth century: the Algerian War. The relationship of Bourdieu's thinking to this event was simultaneously historical, substantive, and critical. His early, formative work unfolded in the context of the French-Algerian conflict. It addressed how the war revealed and perpetuated the politicization of social values associated with subjectivism and objectivism and the detrimental effects of that politicization for the Algerian people. Finally, Bourdieu's early work entailed a study of the relationship between Algerian society and the war as the basis for thinking about social organization in ways that rendered problematic an uncritical acceptance of those values as coherent and univocal. To reassess the challenge of Bourdieu's ambiguity in light of the Algerian War not only affords the opportunity for a more expansive reading of his theoretical originality. It also promises new ways of thinking differently about the significance of the event.

Habitus

As was the case with other mid-twentieth-century French intellectuals, Bourdieu pursued a critique of philosophy and the social sciences and, more specifically, of the claim that the analytic categories associated with these disciplines provided a transparent description or representation of the relationship between individual and society. That critique focused on the binary between what scholars considered to be the two competing categories of social description and understanding: subjectivism and objectivism. Bourdieu did not aim at denying the reality of characteristics commonly associated with subjectivity or structural determinism. Rather, he sought to reveal the specific contextual or historical conditions that produced an insistence on subjectivism or objectivism as unquestionable totalistic forms and to grasp their symbolic role in establishing specific relations of power so as to appreciate the more complex, because "real," interplay of individual action and structural constraint in the making and transformation of everyday social life. Bourdieu attempted to capture this interplay of individual (subjective) action and structural constraint through an understanding of habitus, the central theoretical innovation of his work. In his formulation of it, habitus constitutes a set of "dispositions," produced by a specific social "field" (such as the structural forces associated with capitalism) and "inclining" individuals to act in accordance with its requirements (Butler 114). The dispositions of the habitus are not determining, since individual enactment of them can have transformative effects for social structures. Embodied rather than expressive of individual agency and will, the dispositions characterizing a habitus escape equally classic conceptions of human subjectivity as timeless or universally applicable. As a category that mediates the opposition between the abstract categories of subjectivism and objectivism and that, in doing so, illuminates the contextual questions of power or politics that produce those categories and the debates that oppose them, Bourdieu intended habitus to afford the possibility, at last, of grasping the complex and various forms of the relationship between individual and society that existed in concrete social situations.

　　　An ambiguity characterizes Bourdieu's formulation of habitus, evident most prominently in his attempt to pose a relationship between—without reconciling into a totalistic or coherent form—the subjective and determining aspects of human social life. Some scholars have embraced this ambiguity. Charles Taylor, for example, regards habitus as a healthy corrective to an excessive (and, in his view, increasingly popular) scholarly commitment to rational choice theory by offering the possibility to "place us in some social space" (52). For other scholars, however, the ambiguity expressed in Bourdieu's conception of habitus constitutes a problem to be resolved, although efforts to specify the problem and its resolution lead in opposite directions. Thus, Craig Calhoun traces the limitations of habitus to an insufficiently developed notion of capitalism in Bourdieu's work (83), while Judith Butler points out that Bourdieu's continuing adherence to Marxist determinism impedes the radical performative potential of habitus (113). My interest here is not to assess the specific claims developed by these scholars, but rather to put into question the philosophical perspective that animates their substantive arguments. For in their insistence on (philosophical) consistency, in their tendency to evaluate the potential of habitus in light of other theoretical systems (Marxism, rational choice theory, performativity), they risk reifying and abstracting—even while insisting on the "real" consequences of their theoretical remarks for politics—a theoretical intervention intended by Bourdieu to challenge the strategic operations of (abstract) philosophical ideas. The sociologist Louis Pinto puts it best: "Is it possible," he asks,

> *to speak of the theoretical gains in Bourdieu's work, and of its contribution to philosophical analysis, without by this very action betraying or contradicting the principle that it contains, whose apparent purpose is to demonstrate the impossibility of separating the sense of theory from its concrete use in the acquisition of knowledge? (95)*

Pinto insists upon a specific perspective—the productive value of a critical relationship between the thinker and the world—that structuralists (and theorists more generally) usually assume but sometimes sacrifice, resulting in theoretical work that can reproduce the reifying categories of individual and social experience they purport to criticize. Pinto's insistence on such an engaged theoretical approach closely follows the ideas of Bourdieu, who placed special emphasis on scholarly self-reflexivity in the endeavor to think critically about the world. Bourdieu developed an understanding of scholarly self-reflexivity largely in relation to professional questions: the need for an awareness of the contextual constraints (both material and symbolic) posed by, or imposed upon, a scholar's discipline. As an example, he invoked the practice of reflexivity to address the inadequate translation of his work from the French academic world to an American context. He pointed out the crucial contextual differences between the integrated "human sciences" in France and the distinct disciplinary boundaries carefully patrolled and defended by American academics; he criticized the tendency among American intellectuals to read his books as "theoretical treatises" because such readings ignored their "properly empirical dimension"; and he went so far as to accuse American scholars of unreflective reading and theorization in "the appearance of radical critique," which according to him amounted to little more than a "comfortable submission to intellectual conformity" ("Concluding" 270).

It is here that Bourdieu's extension of this practice of reflexivity to an analysis of the Algerian War—that is, the war as an event—enables us to grasp the significance of habitus. Such an approach seems productive for two reasons. It acknowledges the engagement of mid-twentieth-century French thinkers with the challenges raised by the war. In turn, it provides an opportunity for understanding how the war might have contributed to critical reflection on the meaning of subjectivism and objectivism. In light of this "event," the ambiguity associated with Bourdieu's conception of habitus might assume new meanings.

The Algerian War

Scholarly reflection on the nature of society emerged during the Algerian War as part of the larger debate over universalism. The conflict over whether Algeria should be independent or remain part of France challenged the integrity of the universalistic vision that had informed the French conquest of Algeria and its assimilation into the framework of the French nation-state. In its uniquely French formulation, universalism premised the attainment of human liberty on the recognition of the abstract qualities common to all individuals, to be realized first within the parameters of the nation-state and spread subsequently, and inexorably, worldwide.[3] Burnished in the crucible of political and social transformation that marked the early years of the French Revolution, the ideal of the abstract individual offered a potent alternative to the hierarchy of social differences that grounded the particularistic social order of the Old Regime. But in the context of the conquest and colonization of Algeria after 1830, references to the ideal of individual abstraction often coexisted with a continued insistence on (and denigration of) the particularity of Algerians, in the process associating the realization of universalism with the kinds of exclusions that it was supposed to eradicate. The reasons for this association are complex and, indeed, impossible to consider separately. They include continued adherence to reductive notions of the biological or cultural inferiority of Algerians, the lingering influence of (neo)mercantilist practices, and a longing for social connection and national wholeness expressed through a relationship to (Algerian) "otherness."[4] However complex the causes appeared, the effects were clear enough to many observers: the invocation of universalism, which envisioned a recognition of the abstract individual as the basis for creating a new community based upon political equality and participation, worked paradoxically to differentiate, disenfranchise, and dehumanize Algerians.[5]

This association of universalistic principles and exclusionary practices begins to explain the difficulties involved in resolving the question of whether Algeria should become independent or remain French. Algerians who participated in the independence movement (and the French who supported their efforts) referred to their disenfranchisement as proof of the limitations of universalism and of the need to replace both legal methods and empty categories with a quest (even if pursued by violent means) for national independence. The French military and colonists, despite the differences that separated them on many issues, viewed this move toward separation and recourse to violence as a threat to republican ideals, as well as a confirmation of the unsuitability of Algerians—at least temporarily—for the responsibilities associated with political enfranchisement; in their view, repression (including torture) in the name of protecting the liberty and integrity of France was justified.

A comprehensive history of the war is not possible here. What seems worth emphasizing, however, is that the conflict over universalism, and especially the recourse to violence in efforts to defend the French promise of individual and national liberty or to challenge the insidious effects of its empty promises, created a unique opportunity for the participation of intellectuals in the political life of France.[6] The question of whether Algeria should be recognized as independent or remain French (and, if so, how Algerians could be integrated into the national community in ways consistent with French principles of liberty and equality) involved prominent intellectuals from a wide variety of disciplines (Sartre, Aron, Camus, Lévi-Strauss) and provided a testing ground for the emergence of a new generation of thinkers (Bourdieu, Fanon). Directed as they were to the debate over the meaning and future of universalism, their intellectual positions are not easily categorized; and, as recourse to violence escalated in response to events (the 1955 Philippeville massacre, de Gaulle's coup d'état in May 1958, and his subsequent call for the separation of Algeria and France), many intellectuals changed their commitments from supporting integration to advocating independence (Shepard).

Intellectuals in favor of a future relationship between France and Algeria drew upon universalistic ideas to situate Algerians in a larger history of human progress or development that privileged individual liberty and political rights as the ultimate goal. To be sure, they disagreed on the specific criteria for integrating Algerians into that history: some argued (conservatively) for an emphasis on educational or technological development, while others, more radically, insisted on the eradication of poverty as the necessary condition for realizing the humanity of Algerians. No matter how they conceived the specific path of progress and development, however, intellectuals supporting a continued relationship between France and Algeria judged the pursuit of Algerian independence as an externally imposed political strategy out of touch with and inimical to the inexorable logic of historical progress. In some cases, intellectuals approached the limits of accepted definitions of universalism without directly challenging its ethos. Camus envisioned a community of Algerians and French that combined political and economic integration with cultural mélange; Sartre, following the lines of Marx's proletarian struggle, linked the Algerian crisis with the larger crisis of capitalism and argued for the independence of Algeria as an important stage in the movement toward a social solidarity of humankind. Arguments in favor of the separation of Algeria and France were similarly wide ranging in substance and political orientation, including Raymond Aron's cautious advocacy of the "real" demographic differences between Algerians and the French, Lévi-Strauss's vision of separating Algeria and France as part of a larger intellectual quest to dissolve the illusory category of "man," and Fanon's insistence that Algerians constituted a nation that deserved recognition, even if such recognition could only be achieved by violent means.

Debate among intellectuals about the future of Algeria was often reduced to a dispute over facts. Accusations pointing to an ignorance of the facts of the history of Algeria and its present predicament flew from every corner of the debate. Ignorance was often blamed on a lack of direct knowledge of Algeria and its inhabitants. But more often, and crucially, intellectuals traced this ignorance to preexisting theoretical commitments that prevented participants in the debate from formulating an accurate assessment of the situation. Intellectuals who supported a continued or more effective assimilation of Algeria within the framework of the French nation-state claimed that their critics had ignored the positive (if still ongoing) social transformations effected by French colonial rule or had incorrectly imagined the specificity of an Algerian "national" experience, as yet unfulfilled because frustrated by the French colonial presence. Advocates of independence pointed out the tendency of their critics to incorrectly summarize Algerians as "Arabs" (so as to better justify their need for French tutelage) and exposed the larger incapacity of universalistic constructs to account for the particular situation of Algeria or to recognize its rights to cultural and political autonomy. In assessing the arguments of their "adversaries," intellectuals emphasized the limitations of employing totalizing abstractions ("culture," "community," "nation") for correctly grasping the relationship between France and Algeria, while at the same time failing to recognize their own reliance on equally theoretical constructs.

This shared recourse to the charge of abstraction betrayed a problematic (because largely uncritical) commitment to universalistic principles. For whether intellectuals supported assimilation, association, or independence, the fact remains that nearly all of them drew upon the same generalizing categories (individual, culture, nation, to name only the most prominent ones) in support of their respective, and often contrasting, positions. In doing so, they failed to account for the centrality of those categories in the exclusionary operations of universalism that had fueled the conflict in the first place.

Bourdieu's The Algerians

Bourdieu's contribution to this debate was both complex and unique and perhaps for that reason has remained underappreciated and understudied. *Agrégé* in philosophy during the Algerian War, Bourdieu was so affected by the conflict that he accepted (against the advice of his advisors) a teaching post at a lycée in Algiers. There, he began work on his first research project, an ethnographic study of the Algerian population, published in 1958 under the title *Sociologie de l'Algérie* (English edition, *The Algerians*). "Ethnography" only hints at the importance of this work. It expresses Bourdieu's decision to distance himself from the abstracting tendencies of philosophy as then practiced in France and mobilized in the debate over the war. But Bourdieu was far from relinquishing an engagement with the issues of subjectivism and objectivism that grounded the place of philosophy in intellectual debates about the war. And while "ethnography" suggests the influence of Lévi-Strauss in his attempt to surpass the limitations of philosophy and its preoccupation with realizing the possibilities of a unitary, universal "man," Bourdieu intended his intervention to address the limitations of generalizations about human experience common to anthropology and philosophy (and other disciplines for that matter). What is distinctive about Bourdieu's intervention is the move away from the discrete questions that had structured the contours of the debate—Are Algerians similar to or different from the French? Should Algeria remain assimilated to France or be granted independence?—toward a more fundamental critique of the operations of abstraction that had given form to these questions. That critique of abstraction addressed the limitations of a recourse to universalism for thinking about the future of Algeria and its relationship to France.

Bourdieu developed a far-reaching critique of abstraction through a scholarly study of the war itself.[7] That choice reveals his appreciation of the ways in which contemporary assessments of the significance of the conflict drew upon, and perpetuated, depictions of Algerian society that were simultaneously banal, stilted, and pernicious. In his view, understandings of the war as "the product of a handful of ringleaders who resorted to compulsion and trickery," or as a struggle between criminality and legality, privileged the explanatory power of subjective states (or human agency) in ways that, paradoxically, refused a recognition of Algerians as subjects (*Algerians* 142–48). Bourdieu attempted to undermine a naive belief in the transparent evidence of subjective states in the unfolding of this particular event by pointing out how the references to a struggle in Algeria ultimately gained expression through the binary opposition between "Europeans" and "Arabs" or "Christians" and "Arabs" (147–48). As an alternative to what he viewed as this uncritical reliance on subjectivity, Bourdieu advocated a consideration of the "social facts" so as to recognize that the "war had its basis in an objective situation" (145). This insistence on an "objective [social] situation," however, did not imply an endorsement of the utility or accuracy of Marxist theory. Bourdieu found the latter as limiting as references to subjective states, especially in the teleological orientation of its emphasis on dialectical social development. Bourdieu distanced himself from Marxist theory by refusing to see the war as "purely and simply a class struggle" (151). What he sought instead was to understand the war as part of a "particular," "specific," and "real" social situation constituted by the "colonial system." Such an approach, Bourdieu maintained, would not rely on abstract categories or schemas as much as it would reveal their political operations. He attempted to accomplish this goal through a study of Algerian society that resisted any reliance on established categories of social analysis.

The importance, for Bourdieu, of grasping a social situation that defied categorical analysis accounts for his detailed depiction of the contours of Algerian society on the eve of its encounter with the French colonial presence. In this depiction Bourdieu carefully avoided conventional summaries of Algeria as a single entity or as a society comprised of discrete, homogeneous groupings. His approach took specific aim against the tendency of scholars to divide the Algerian population into Kabyles and Arabs, two opposing groups that, writ small, were often invoked to represent the struggle between the promise of civilization and the obstacle of barbarism that informed the colonial project and that found its fulfillment in the war. (Colonial studies of the Algerian population depicted the Kabyle as sedentary, blond, democratic, and thus as both open and capable of assimilating to European/Christian/capitalist values; Arabs, nomadic and loyal to Koranic law, embodied the retrograde characteristics that needed to be overcome in order for humanistic values to be fully realized).[8] Bourdieu amended these conventional understandings of the Algerian population with a needed dose of diversification. He included not only Jews but also groups like the Mozabites, who lived according to distinctive, particular configurations of Islamic values and practices (37–50).

Central to the depiction of this diversification was Bourdieu's refusal to assign exclusive and defining characteristics to specific groupings. Nomadic ways of life are evident among the Kabyles, while Arabs are often sedentary. Mozabite Arabs have formed a way of life distinct from other Muslims, a strategy that protects their dissident status, while some "Jews" share with "Arabs" the cult of the saints and even adopt "simultaneous or successive polygamy" (93). Bourdieu employed the evidence of shared values and practices to identify cultural interaction as the law or principle that governs the existence of social groupings in Algeria. Cultural interaction makes sense of how sedentary and nomadic practices do not simply coexist but are interdependent and explains why, despite their specific contours, specific groups adopt common values and practices such as the social organization of the clan. Bourdieu enhanced, and further complicated, his understanding of the salience of cultural interaction in the lives of Algerians by denying any role for strict causal determinism in the formation of group identities, values, practices, and interaction. In place of determinism, he posited a reciprocal influence, tending toward the establishment of equilibrium, between the various aspects of human (physical, economic, social, cultural) experience. The best example that Bourdieu provided of this complexity is the Mozabites, "the Protestants and Puritans of Islam" (38). He argued that their collective identification as dissident Muslims could not be explained causally, that is, as a direct expression of and reaction to challenges posed by their living conditions. Rather, Bourdieu insisted, a self-conscious attempt by Mozabites to protect their dissident way of life originally led them to search out a harsh climate, while their particular (Islamic) way of life in turn enabled them to endure and thrive in these conditions. For other "Arab-speaking peoples,"[9] life in a harsh climate might not have been so explicitly chosen. But neither did such conditions determine their social structures and cultural practices, for climate called into being ways of life that allowed various "Arab speaking peoples" to adapt, live, and evolve in specific circumstances. The elaboration of those ways of life also accounts for specific religious identifications and economic practices, which should not be viewed as any more determining than climate (as was the case in conventional references to a monolithic "Islam" or the rigors of economic backwardness).

What is important to understand here is how Bourdieu's depiction of Algerian social organization as complex, malleable, and indeterminate placed in an entirely new light the opposing (that is, ostensibly "positive" and "negative") representations that shaped the debate over the significance of the war as an event. Whether these representations denied Algeria the status of a society and Algerians the capability of individual subjectivity, maintained the possibility of individual liberty and equality contingent on future social development, or insisted on the status of Algeria as an independent nation, they linked a consideration of the humanity of Algerians to French influence and intervention. In contrast, Bourdieu's emphasis on complexity and malleability portrays Algerian society simply as vital and thus as deserving of being considered "human" on its own terms (63, 110). The recognition of this vitality at once grounds the ambiguity of Bourdieu's social analysis and casts that ambiguity productively and positively. For the vitality of society manifested in cultural "ways of life" where everything is "inseparably joined and connected, and consequently everything is at the same time cause and effect," escapes the demeaning and violent effects of representation (50). (As one example of this, Bourdieu cites the Mozabites, whose vibrant religious culture not only allows them to thrive in harsh climatic conditions but also enables them to engage in modern economic practices without relinquishing their traditional religious devotion [50]). But the vitality of Algerian society that secures the status of the human, paradoxically, eludes full comprehension. Such is the cost, in Bourdieu's view, of acknowledging and criticizing the political operations of representation.

Bourdieu's emphasis on the vital character of Algerian culture made it impossible to take seriously the status of "Islam," "nomad," "sedentary," or "class" (among others) as categories of transparent description or representation. That is not to say that Bourdieu denied their existence, so much as he redeployed them in a very different understanding of what was at stake in the Algerian War. Bourdieu put aside conventional interpretations of the French colonial endeavor in Algeria, which focused on the importance of capitalist development and hegemony or the misguided extension of universalistic principles. Even as they might reveal, in different ways, the destructive aims and effects of the colonial endeavor, these lines of interpretation left untouched the appearance of the social coherence of colonialism, an appearance confirmed and secured through references to the analytic categories of rights, equality, class, ideology, and so on. Instead, Bourdieu detected in the French reliance on the abstract opposition between civilization and barbarism, or aspirations for social development, a demonstration of the social aporia that existed at the heart of the French colonial enterprise. French colonists, cut off from any meaningful relationship with France, engaged in "conservative" economic activities like winegrowing and, lacking substantive social relations more generally, fashioned an identity for themselves through a differentiation from—and a negation of—the "traditional" Algerian social order. In this fantasy of abstraction, Bourdieu argued, the Algerian is made to feel the stranger. To view the effects of this identity formation, which resulted most prominently in the production of a pronounced "caste system," as destructive of Algerian social order or as racist or both is at once to get and miss the point. For the formation of this identity brought together, in an incoherent yet destructive manner, various principles—assimilation, association, humanitarianism, emancipation, social development, policing of subversives—that Bourdieu's intellectual peers (as do scholars today) referred to and attempted to separate (so as to clarify) in their efforts to understand the reality of Algeria and its future possibilities. Bourdieu revealed the empty yet dangerous power of these confused categories by insisting, for example, upon the continuity between the nineteenth-century codification of rules for the confiscation of Algerian communal property and the massive relocations of millions of Kabyles during the war (1954–60). To facilitate this relocation, the French built makeshift villages, furnished with the requisite school, bar, city hall, war memorial, and uniform lodgings: in short, "dead cities" that continued the social destruction begun by expropriation and whose aims found completion in the violence of the war.[10]

The consequences of the deployment of these abstract categories for the vibrancy of Algerian culture, as Bourdieu portrays them, appear dire indeed. Not surprisingly, Bourdieu, ever vigilant against the all too easy and demeaning conclusions to be drawn from either an uncritical embrace or naive rejection of the power of representational categories, provides more ambiguous conclusions. At times, his depiction of Algerian ways of life transformed by the destructive force of French colonialism—proletarian peasants who no longer express an attachment to the land (now belonging to the French) even as they work it, peasants for whom rural proletarianization has enabled a continued but "fictive" attachment to traditional routines, peasants who become workers in urban centers but who sustain an agricultural identity by returning regularly to their farms—suggests an out-of-touch or "pathological" condition at odds with the precolonial vibrancy of Algerian culture (68). At other times, he presents transformed Algerian ways of life as a complex and "lived" reaction—a *prise de conscience*—that challenged, by embodying, the contradictions of a colonial intervention in its attempt to realize civilization through the intertwined processes of objectifying and destroying traditional social structures and values. Included among these "new" and ambiguous ways of life is the transformation of the veil from the merely "vestimentary" to something endowed with an essence[11] and the transition from the destruction of older solidarities to the formation of new ones.

The ambiguity expressed by Bourdieu's refusal to state "categorically" the significance of the reactions of Algerians to the experience of colonization and the war, and what they might portend for the future, resonates with his earlier presentation of the vitality of Algerian culture. It also reinforces connections between his "ambiguous" presentation of that culture and his perception of the limitations of abstract, categorical analysis that, implicated in the French colonization of Algeria (including the war), could not be consequently invoked to explain it. Bourdieu expressed his reservations about a definitive explanation of the war and its effects when he asked his readers in *Le Déracinement*: "Is such an object not a challenge to scientific analysis and are we not doomed to crash together descriptions that are just as contradictory as the object described?"[12] Thus, Bourdieu refused to link Algeria's future to the established or authoritative socialist visions (those of Sartre and Fanon, for example) (171). In his view, those visions offered a coherent and comprehensive appraisal of the Algerian situation only by embracing a partial and ossified representation of reality and its future. Just as Bourdieu sought to situate a new understanding of the war in a more critically acute portrayal of Algerian society—a portrayal that would not only escape the simplicity of explanatory categories but could also expose those categories for what they were—so, too, he sought a social (socialist?) program for the future of Algerians attuned to the concrete details of their social situation and lives (176).

Bourdieu began this quest through a study of the "event" of the Algerian war of independence. Existing representations of that event had all too easily confounded historical evidence, specific political aims, and references to the human. But Bourdieu's savvy, elusive study of Algeria demonstrates that a quest for the significance of an event, when pursued from a critical perspective cognizant and wary of established links between the study of events and the production of norms, might accomplish some real good. In the context of Algeria, this would involve the inclusion of various and unexpected configurations of what are commonly opposed as "tradition" and "modernity," such as the wedding of secular principles and religious values or of capitalist development and local social practices.

ANDREW AISENBERG is Associate Professor of History at Scripps College. He is the author of *Contagion: Disease, Government, and the "Social Question" in Nineteenth-Century France* (Stanford University Press, 1999).

Notes

1 See esp. Bourdieu's *Outline of a Theory of Practice* and *The Logic of Practice*.

2 Two indispensable collections of essays devoted to an evaluation of Bourdieu's work are Shusterman's *Bourdieu: A Critical Reader* and Calhoun et al.'s *Bourdieu: Critical Perspectives*.

3 See Condorcet.

4 See Lorcin; Marseille; and Wilder.

5 See Scott.

6 My analysis in the following pages draws upon James Le Sueur.

7 His focus on the war is both implicit (xi) and explicit, as in "Revolution within the Revolution." The latter first appeared as an article in *La nouvel*

observateur. It was subsequently included as the concluding chapter of *The Algerians.*

8 See ch. 1, "The Kabyle," in *The Algerians*. See also Lorcin, "Scholarly Societies in France," in *Imperial Identities*.

9 This is the title of chapter 4 of *The Algerians*.

10 For a comprehensive analysis of this resettlement, see Bourdieu and Sayad.

11 See *The Algerians* 156 and *Le Déracinement* 132.

12 "Un tel objet n'est-il pas un défi à l'analyse scientifique et n'est-on pas condamné à entrechoquer des descriptions aussi contradictoires que l'objet décrit?" (162).

Works Cited

Bourdieu, Pierre. *The Algerians*. Rev. ed. Boston: Beacon P, 1961.

——————. "Concluding Remarks: For a Sociogenetic Understanding of Intellectual Works." Calhoun et al. 263–75.

——————. *The Logic of Practice*. Stanford: Stanford UP, 1992.

——————. *Outline of a Theory of Practice*. Cambridge: Cambridge UP, 1977.

——————. *Sociologie de l'Algérie*. 1958. 8th ed. Paris: Presses universitaires de France, 2006.

Bourdieu, Pierre, and Abdelmalek Sayad. *Le Déracinement: La crise de l'agriculture traditionnelle en Algérie*. Paris: Minuit, 2004.

Butler, Judith. "Peformativity's Social Magic." Shusterman 113–28.

Calhoun, Craig. "Habitus, Field and Capital: The Question of Historical Specificity." Calhoun et al. 60–88.

Calhoun, Craig, Edward LiPuma, and Moishe Postone, eds. *Bourdieu: Critical Perspectives.* Chicago: U of Chicago P, 1993.

Condorcet, Marie Jean Antoine de. *Sketch for a Historical Picture of the Progress of the Human Mind.* Trans. June Barraclough. Westport: Hyperion, 1955.

Le Sueur, James D. *Uncivil War: Intellectuals and Identity Politics during the Decolonization of Algeria.* Lincoln: U of Nebraska P, 2001.

Lorcin, Patricia M. E. *Imperial Identities: Stereotyping, Prejudice, and Race in Colonial Algeria.* London: I. B. Tauris, 1999.

Marseille, Jacques. *Empire colonial et capitalisme français: Histoire d'un divorce.* Paris: A. Michel, 1984.

Pinto, Louis. "Theory in Practice." Shusterman 94–112.

Scott, Joan Wallach. *The Politics of the Veil.* Princeton: Princeton UP, 2007.

Sewell, William H., Jr. *Logics of History: Social Theory and Social Transformation.* Chicago: U of Chicago P, 2005.

Shepard, Todd. *The Invention of Decolonization.* Ithaca: Cornell UP, 2006.

Shusterman, Richard, ed. *Bourdieu: A Critical Reader.* London: Wiley-Blackwell, 1999.

Taylor, Charles. "To Follow a Rule." Calhoun et al. 45–60.

Thompson, E. P. *The Making of the English Working Class.* London: Vintage, 1966.

Wilder, Gary. *The French Imperial Nation-State: Negritude and Colonial Humanism between the Two World Wars.* Chicago: U of Chicago P, 2005.

The Era of Lost (White) Girls: On Body and Event

There is nothing particularly unusual about [LaToyia Figueroa's] case. She is an inner-city African-American/Latino woman, living a more than unconventional lifestyle in a high crime area, and now she's missing—big surprise [. . .]. The Natalee Holloway case is national news. She is a beautiful young woman, with a full scholarship to the University of Alabama, who disappears on what would otherwise be a dream vacation to an island resort with the lowest crime rate in the world [. . .]. No one cares about the LaToyia Figueroa case because it has nothing to do with the lives of 88 percent of the American public.
—Mike, posting to the *SkaroffBlog*

Those who are racially marginalized are like the miner's canary: their distress is the first sign of a danger that threatens us all.
—Guinier and Torres

Washington Post columnist Eugene Robinson suggests that when historians discuss "the decade bracketing the turn of the twenty-first century," they will identify "Damsels in Distress" as one of the major themes engrossing the country ("[White]"A23). Names such as JonBenét Ramsey, Megan Kanka, Elizabeth Smart, Natalee Holloway, and Laci Peterson entered the cultural lexicon during this period, so famous that their first names alone could trigger the stories of their victimization in many citizens' minds.[1] Their disappearances and murders have been made into media and cultural events. Transforming local tragedies into national events has required certain consistent narrative markers; these victims have white skin, gender, and certain depicted characteristics in common. Words such as "perfect," "ideal," "angelic," "golden," and "fairy tale" are used in the media to describe them or their lives, and such labels are essential to the reification that takes place after their disappearance.

Volume 19, Number 2   DOI 10.1215/10407391-2008-005
© 2008 by Brown University and d i f f e r e n c e s : A Journal of Feminist Cultural Studies

They are perpetually *girls* in media narratives because what happens to girls is described as "every parent's worst nightmare." When children grow up, their subject positions can become more complex and the narratives of their lives more complicated; thus the narratives of ideality required for national media attention are greatly facilitated when victims are portrayed as angelic children. These idealized victims are simultaneously every child and unique signifiers of the risks facing all girls. Commonsense logic might suggest that narratives drawing attention to violence against women and children are politically useful, even if only certain kinds of citizens are presented as poster children. However, this recurring media spectacle, which we might call the Lost Girl Event in U.S. culture, comes at the significant political cost of mischaracterizing what places most citizens at risk. The Lost Girl Event is always about innocent girls, inexplicable violence, and villainy. Ironically, tales about the missing and murdered girls lost through unnatural occurrences make cozy bedfellows of psychological comfort and cultural anxiety. It may seem counterintuitive to suggest that stories about the abduction, rape, and murder of children could provide any kind of comfort. Nevertheless, these horrific stories do offer some comfort because the multiheaded hydra of the most significant causes of child mortality and abuse would require more nuanced storytelling.

Stranger abduction tops parents' concerns but is one of the least likely dangers to children in the United States (Glassner 66). While the majority of child deaths are from unintentional injury, child mortality could be greatly reduced by addressing the reality that millions of children lack health insurance, thousands of infants die from low birth weight (and most of these are born into poverty), and the majority of children killed are murdered by people they know.[2] When the abduction of idealized girls becomes the sign of the most significant risk facing the nation, the villains are more easily identified and the complex problems that require multipronged solutions are subjugated to more comforting stories about individual bad actors. The Lost Girl body is reconfigured and imbued with more meaning than she can possibly hold, becoming a powerful symbol through the carefully crafted representation of her disappearance or death. She becomes not only the ideal girl but the ideal citizen that the nation's policies are designed to protect. This slippage between child and citizen is, as Lauren Berlant has explained, foundational to much of U.S. political rhetoric (1).[3] Making these abductions into national events involves transforming not only bodies into ideals but the nation into a place where children were once safe. The stories of the "other" citizens (those who lack the visibility afforded by iconographic individualistic fables) challenge racialized notions of who can count as a Lost Citizen by demanding tales that remain attentive to context and eschewing lyricism for statistics, thus putting pressure on a cultural disregard of citizens who do not fit the ideal. Moreover, such stories neglect the needs of citizens who might fit the ideal but are still at risk for harms that occur more frequently than abduction. Lost Girl Events rely upon an ideological framework in the United States that ignores the consistent and systemic neglect of some lost citizens, citizens who, if made into events, would challenge national discourses about who can represent the nation.

The difference between the lost citizen and the Lost Girl is actually integral to the construction of the Lost Girl Event because other kinds of citizens define the parameters for the ideal. In the traditional discourses of race, gender, and sexuality in the United States, what is Eva without Topsy, or the "lady" without the "whore"? The media began to recognize the disparity in event-making in a few twenty-first-century cases, typically through contrasting cases about African American lost girls and Lost (White) Girl Events. While a critique of the Lost Girl Event could focus on gender or class disparities, I shall focus on the neglect of stories about lost African American girls because national discussions of their treatment have most prominently illustrated the reasons that the loss of some citizens do not become events. Their bodies stand as the excessive other to the golden purity of Lost (White) Girls. If the devalued black girl body did not exist, those who make Lost (White) Girl Events would have to invent her.

Spectacular stories about abducted and murdered girls in u.s. culture possess three characteristics that encode them as national events: the transformation of the murdered into abstract signs of the nation's idealized past and anxieties about the nation's future; an overemphasis on innocence as a condition of cultural value; and a dialectical relationship to others, such as African Americans, whose cultural circumstances challenge the fantasies offered by the Lost Girl narrative. If advocates for lost citizens wish to intervene in Lost Girl discourse, they must combat the conventions undergirding these narratives. Lost Girls must be fairy-tale heroines, golden in visage and character, offering bodies that can sustain a fairy-tale ending for others, even when the ending for the specific lost girl is a terrible death. The Lost Girl must be able to represent the fairy-tale ending imagined as a possible future for the idealized child in the United

States, those protected after the villains are caught. Lost Girl Events are thus stories of fairy tales disrupted, and state action is warranted precisely insofar as it is seen as enabling the possibility of an uninterrupted fairy-tale life within a nuclear family and the propagation of more ideal children. It thus perpetuates the myth that fewer children will be lost if we catch and incarcerate more individual bad actors. But for the Lost Girl Event to have this recuperative meaning, its antithesis, the nonevent, must always be a shadowy presence. To illuminate that shadow—the nonevent body, the body that cannot figure this utopia—is to shed light on the reasons why the Lost Girl is always the Lost (White) Girl. As Gilles Deleuze explains in his theory of the event, "The Other is initially a structure of the perceptual field, without which the entire field could not function as it does" (307). The Lost Girl Event is defined by the others in the U.S. imaginary. Their existence is antithetical to the premises of fairy tales, their bodies are perpetually at risk. Many lost citizens never achieve the status of events, largely because they force a narrative about the more complex issues—such as poverty—that need to be addressed in order to make both children and adults safer.

On Bodies and Time

Over the last twenty years, parents, media, and activists have been preoccupied with the abduction and murder of white girls in the United States, but the preoccupation with child abduction is not an entirely new national obsession. As Paula S. Fass recounts in her history of prominent child abduction cases in the United States, the victims were boys in the earliest high-profile abductions and murders of children in the United States, and they could largely be described as "golden boys" who either were from wealthy backgrounds or appeared to be so. Assuredly, many children were abducted and murdered by strangers throughout U.S. history, but as Fass explains, "The issue of child kidnapping" has been "most vividly represented in stories of specific lost and missing children" (9). Her history looks at how the abduction of specific children shaped national discourse in given eras, and she argues that telling the story through the loss of individual children "is most true to our experience of the problem" (9). While Fass is right to point to the relationship between body and historical moment in making these abductions into events, the "our" in Fass's articulation of national experience capitulates to a homogeneous national history. The history of national discussions of kidnapping should include Indian captivity narratives, Indian removal, and the selling of children during chattel slavery. While individuals have told stories about experiencing these abductions, the phenomenon has been best explained through the story of collective harms, rather than through individual heroism, victimization, and villainy. Thus while Fass is right that the kidnapping narrative in the United States is often made manifest in national stories about the loss of a particular child, her claim masks the larger ideological underpinning of making the lost child into a national event. Most significantly, she obscures the role that race plays in complicating more simplistic stories about abduction. Even as the loss of a particular child is mapped onto larger narratives about u.s. culture, this mapping offers the comfort that such abductions are aberrations in the lives of u.s. children. Fass's capitulation to this argument means that the Atlanta Child Murders, the kidnapping and deaths of an unprecedented twenty-nine children and young adults between 1979 and 1981, warrant only a brief mention in her account. While this is an event that caught the attention of the u.s. public and terrified the national black population, the complexity of those murders was difficult to attribute to a lone evildoer or single bad cause, even as an individual black actor was ultimately and controversially blamed for all of the murders.[4] Child abductions that are narrated as national events resist complexity, as those who tell the stories cast about for a singular narrative solution that would make sense of unspeakable acts.

If we understand that stories of abducted and murdered children in the United States are beholden to more general practices of national storytelling that privilege the individual as universal rather than focusing on the collective, then the ways in which the horror of child murder can be mobilized into a narrative of comfort becomes more apparent. Such a transformation is perhaps nowhere so evident as in the story of Megan Kanka, whose murder became one of the most significant abduction events of the late twentieth century, even though many people do not know her full name. Kanka is best known as the body mapped onto the piece of legislation called Megan's Law, which requires the registration of convicted sex offenders. The story of how Megan became cemented in the national imagination demonstrates what discursively happens to a body transformed by violence into event and also illustrates how a grisly, atypical death can become representative of widespread risks.

Megan Kanka's story—and stories like hers—depend on first presenting an idealized space and life that is interrupted. A columnist thus describes Kanka's parents as "raising her in a quiet neighborhood of neat homes in New Jersey, the kind of place in which neighbors often know one another" (Quindlen 19), where parents do not worry when their kids are out of sight because it is "such a nice neighborhood."[5] However, they did not know the backgrounds of all their neighbors, and on a summer day in 1994, Megan was walking home from a friend's when the "promise of [a] puppy lured her to [her] death" (Lutton). While her parents had told her not to talk to strangers, she probably thought it was acceptable to talk to Jesse Timmendequas, the neighbor across the street, who, unbeknownst to her, was a convicted sex offender. The prosecutor of her murderer describes her walking into the house "unsuspecting" and "trusting"; her body was later found in some bushes a few miles away. This "great little girl," her mother said, was treated "like she was a piece of trash" (Jerome and Eftimiades).

What eventually became of the story of Megan Kanka's murder illustrates how a domestic trauma becomes a local event and how a local event can be transformed into a national one. The murder of children almost always warrants status as a local event: this is a rupture that registers on the lives of a community, moving beyond the status of a domestic trauma. A local event may cause only a momentary rupture, registering in the local news for one to a few days. Such events interpellate individuals in a paradoxical way by evoking both the clearly imagined and familiar—the child's innocence—and the unimaginable horror of something that most citizens can only partially envision and do not want to see too clearly. However, it is the tension between cultural narratives that define everyday anxiety and those that trigger unnatural or excessive anxiety that sustains event status, producing the conditions that constitute a national event. While illness and car accidents are possible for everyone, the trauma that is described as unlikely and atypical but harbors the possibility of becoming everyday transforms the shelf life of an event. These kinds of events destabilize cultural stories, transforming the narratives that many citizens tell about their pasts, presents, and futures.

From the minute the general public learned the facts of her death, Megan Kanka became fragmented into before and after. News stories constantly told about her past, a past narrowed to encompass only the moment of her death in the national imagination. Thus when a legislator evokes the "memory of Megan," he refers exclusively to her death and the law that memorializes her loss. Trauma transforms her body in time so that the Megan before her murder is always read in relationship to her murder and the aftermath. While her parents, family, and friends know more about this "great little girl," her life story is condensed into a single moment of time. But Megan is most strongly cemented in the national imagination because of the future she will never have. Her mother mourns and wonders: "You always think about what she would look like. What would she be doing, would she be out with her friends, would she have a boyfriend?" (Mothers). However, the future imagined is not only Megan's missing years but the collective futures of other children. One newspaper editorial frames this cultural response as a "fierce" and angry feeling that "something must be done—fast and bold—to save the next Megan" ("On Barbara"). Megan's murdered self, her thwarted future self, and the imagined futures of others combine to make Lost Girl Megan, trapped in time and setting the terms for the future her advocates would like to imagine. As Deleuze explains, the pure event possesses a slippery relationship to time: "In its impassability and impenetrability," it

> has no present. It rather retreats and advances in two directions at once, being the perpetual object of a double question. What is going to happen? What has just happened? The agonizing aspect of the pure event is that it is always and at the same time something which has just happened and something about to happen; never something which is happening. (63)

Thus an event "eludes the present" largely through the language and narration that position it in both the past and the future. This temporal shiftiness ultimately leads to essential building blocks in the construction of meaning: the loss of personal identity that imposes the incorporealization of a body as an effect. A body becomes effect; it becomes something that has had something happen to it and is thus incorporealized. Deleuze thus describes *Alice's Adventures in Wonderland* as a story about what happened to Alice and not as a story about Alice per se. To realize this is to acknowledge a melancholy state of affairs: that the story of what happens to a subject displaces the subject. The fact that we may all be lost in the stories we tell about ourselves may be a general existential crisis, but what I want to explicitly argue is that when a rarified body is lost through violence, it causes anxiety about past, present, and future, thereby disrupting what Priscilla Wald would call the "official stories" that a nation needs to maintain its ideological coherence (2).

When Megan Kanka became a Lost Girl, she served a role in the stories about idealized childhoods that the nation tells about such girls. When she was murdered, the unexpected rupture of the event transformed her into something other than the already overdetermined idealized American white girl. She became the raped and murdered child Megan. What Deleuze would describe as the linguistic purity of her proper name is destroyed by the event of the rape. Megan is rewritten as "what happened to Megan," "how do we survive what happened to Megan," "how do we punish Megan's murderer?" Part of the harm done by the murder is the damage done to the possibility of memory; Megan can never again be remembered without the event of her death being the determining event of her life. Such a rupture creates a domestic and sometimes local event, but the national event emerges when the anxiety produced by her fragmentation into Murdered Megan is read as a rupture to national ideology. When the rupture is constructed as possible every day and as conceivably impacting some citizen constructed as "average," the local trauma can become a national event.

Affect is the engine that transforms incident into event. Citizens imagine Megan's emotions and the emotions of her loved ones who survive her. But what makes the event into a national event is its "agonizing aspect," the transformation of local temporal uncertainty—Megan and her loved ones—into national temporal unrest. As columnist Anna Quindlen describes it: "I am left with a feeling. It is the feeling you get when you think of a 7-year-old being raped. It is part revulsion, part rage, as real as a high fever" (19). While personal trauma is marked by mourning who Megan was and by questions about what she suffered and what will happen to her perpetrator and those who survive her loss, the national event is marked by mourning the possibility of similar losses, by anxiety about when, where, and how similar events might occur. Perhaps most importantly, trauma cast as a national event is marked by the insistence that this is a *new* anxiety about what will become of a nation that must live with the threat of such events. The organization Mothers against Predators describes the alleged newness of child predators on its website: "Sexual abuse is rarely discussed among adults or children, until recently the problem was left alone. The problem is that it *now* exists in our neighborhoods and in our every day way of life. Sexual abuse has come to the forefront" (my emphasis). The trauma that becomes a national event must be accompanied by a story that emphasizes its simultaneous newness and omnipresence. The event is something that has always been present but was masked, something that has been allowed to erupt, shattering the fantasy of an idyllic past. The national event is a story encompassing a collective past and possible future, a fable with a moral. Pure events are, as Deleuze argues, both "tale and novella, never and actuality" (63).

Part of the tale is Megan's Law, which is more about the story the nation would like to tell about children at risk than about the complexities of what causes them harm. The creation of Megan's Law is an effort to stabilize the temporal unrest with a singular solution. The sex offender registration law named for Megan Kanka proposes that children can be protected if the public knows that sex offenders are among their neighbors. However, as many critics have argued, this proposition masks the much greater risks posed by those intimates—neighbors, friends, and family members—well known to children. Megan's Law offers the fantasy of an end to the uncertainty produced by the event of her murder. Events are perpetual and unending, and the law quickly became part of the event, ensuring the perpetuity of Megan's murder in cultural memory even as it gestures to the possibility of ending anxiety and preventing another such death.

Megan Kanka's transformation into the Lost Girl Event illustrates some of the possible perils in the transformation of body into event. Reification and temporal anxiety are the inevitable consequences of the body transformed by trauma, but such results do not make the event created by lost bodies inherently problematic. While it is tragic that we cannot know more about Megan's life than her death, it is not the fragmentation of the body or even the anxiety it produces that makes the Lost Citizen event troubling. It is the specific result of reification and the kind of temporal anxieties it spawns that make the Lost Girl Event politically disingenuous. Because Megan was transformed into the representative ideal of innocent girlhood whose idyllic childhood was cut short (in a neighborhood where parents do not worry), the discourse around her body privileges harms to those who are imagined as having ideal lives and communities. I do not question Megan's innocence or the tragedy of her loss. But the cost of privileging the ideal is the erasure of more widespread harms. Even in the case of Megan's death, the meaning of her loss could have been transformed into something else. What if her loss was not about the predatory stranger invading the ideal neighborhood, evoking the "war on predators" rhetoric of Lost Girl Events? What if we framed the loss in terms of the everyday risk posed by those whom children know? If we reposition Jesse Timmendequas—who Kanka had assuredly seen before—as familiar and not as a stranger? It may be impossible to stop making murdered bodies into events, given the titillation that murders provide. But we can put pressure on what the body comes to signify and interrogate the choice of particular bodies over others.

Innocence and Lost Girls

The media began to question their investment in white girl-hood, and the innocence it is made to signify, in two moments in the early twenty-first century. The first moment was a small fissure in the jugger-naut of Lost Girl Event storytelling, raised by a reporter who was frustrated that a lost girl from his city, Alexis Patterson, did not receive as much attention as "angelic" Elizabeth Smart, who disappeared during the same period in 2002. The second moment followed a seemingly endless cycle of Lost Girl Events over the next three years—a pregnant woman murdered by her adulterous husband, young white girls murdered by pedophiles, an eighteen-year-old who disappeared in Aruba on a class trip, and per-haps most infamously, the "Runaway Bride," who faked an abduction and claimed that a Mexican man and his girlfriend had kidnapped her.[6] The media appeared to be following, with slight modification, the aesthetic mandates of Edgar Allan Poe, who famously wrote that the "death of a beautiful woman is unquestionably the most poetical topic in the world." Poe's dead women—always of alabaster skin—become monsters them-selves, and his narratives blend the source of beauty, pleasure, and terror. In these real-life horror stories, the blend of horror and beauty is in the event itself—Girl Murder. As former reporter for Court TV, Terry Moran, explains in his condemnation of media coverage inequities, "[T]rue life tales-of-terror warm our hearts [. . .]. So we have made a modern bogeyman to keep us close, to make us thankful for the haven of our troubled homes as we turn out the lights. Murder is our plague, our famine, our blight. It is the tale we tell ourselves to frighten our hearts into loving well" (C1). Moran's indictment of inequitable media coverage powerfully highlights the challenge facing those confronting the "national disgrace" of the media determination that certain stories are unimportant: "Stories mean more than statistics." Thus the massive number of children murdered in the 1980s from violent crime—largely black—and the children in the pres-ent whose deaths are in fact more representative of the risk facing more children do not receive what Moran describes as "the kind of sustained, textured storytelling that many news organizations have served up in the epic murder cases of the past few years" (C1).

The idea that lost white girls make better stories implies that storytelling is organic to an event. Shaping the sensational into an event representative of the risks facing the most citizens actually requires storytelling that masks the representative nature of many harms. Such storytelling eschews the possibility that the everyday can be made sensational. A comparison of the media surrounding Alexis Patterson and Elizabeth Smart illustrates the fallacies of the media's storytelling logic. In 2002, a blonde and blue-eyed fourteen-year-old girl named Elizabeth Smart was abducted from her bed in Salt Lake City. Her image and story were ubiquitous—she was constantly pictured with her affluent, Mormon family or playing a harp. The "no. 1 description of her" was "angelic," and "by all accounts, if fourteen-year-old Elizabeth Smart has a fault it's that she doesn't have any" (Benson B1). While no new details could be added to the tale of her disappearance, the media continued to circulate her story endlessly. One of the miraculous results of her constant media presence was her recovery—someone who recognized her reported the sighting, and Smart was reunited with her parents in 2003. In contrast, the face of seven-year-old Alexis Patterson had no national narrative value. Disappearing in Milwaukee a month before Smart was abducted on May 3, 2002, she was substantially less affluent, African American, and never recovered (Jurkowitz). Her stepfather had dropped her off near her school, and she disappeared somewhere between the car and the school door. One resident of Salt Lake City claimed that Smart's abduction was shocking because "[t]hings like that didn't happen here" (Waxman A3), whereas "whatever happens in a black neighborhood doesn't really surprise anybody" (Dougherty B6). Patterson's disappearance was depicted as a distressing but predictable outcome of identity and location; she was a statistic and Smart a story.

While Megan Kanka's reification resulted in fragmentation into an ideal innocence or innocence lost, Patterson's reification results in her being mapped onto uncompelling numbers. The national media could make a sensation of such a story—how many children are dropped off at school by their parents? How much would it terrify parents to think of their children disappearing in the short moment between the time their child leaves the car and arrives at the door to the school? Patterson's disappearance could be just as much an unrepresentative bogeyman as Smart's abduction, but the other ways in which Patterson could be at risk negate the possible sensationalism of her loss. While Smart's abduction was constructed as unthinkable, Patterson's possessed a kind of inevitability. The binary oppositions between all-American girls and those never configured as such; between the white nuclear family and an allegedly dysfunctional lower class; between undeserved white suffering and self-inflicted black suffering are not new in American culture. As Robert M. Entman and Andrew Rojecki have documented, blacks are not constructed as an American "us" in the news media. They are the anti-ideal whose suffering is presumed as given because of their contexts—even though complex contextual explanations for black victimization or crime are rarely provided. Contexts require story, not only statistics, and yet quantitative data are essential to presenting the scope of tragedy. However, statistics dehumanize and, perhaps, ungender Patterson in u.s. cultural logic. As a black girl victimized by violence, she can cease to be a girl. If African American girls and their families are seen as always already bringing it on themselves or as faceless numbers, their victimization is encoded in a way that can ungender them in the u.s. imagination. In a tradition that Hortense Spillers explains began in the Middle Passage, African American female bodies are often unmade by both violence against them and the discourse that sees them as bodies that can be treated with violence (72). This cultural unmaking contributes to the naturalization of the Lost (White) Girl Event at the expense of other kinds of bodies.

Because African American girls are not the only kind of bodies devalued in the Lost Girl Event, I want to emphasize that they are only hypervisible examples of the counterideal in u.s. culture. The example of ignored lost black girls is implicated in the broader cultural logic of child-as-citizen protection. Capitulating to the logic produced about marketability naturalizes an American Dream fantasy with certain kinds of children at its center, a fantasy that treats the disruptions of white innocence as singular ruptures. These disruptions stand in stark contrast to the constant attacks endured by not only black girl children but many other citizens at risk. The logic undergirding abduction narratives in twenty-first-century culture are as follows: (1) our children are our most valuable resource and they must be protected; (2) single, irredeemably evil actors kill our girls; and (3) their ability to prey on our children and women is often a result of a criminal justice system that protects criminals to the detriment of the innocent, thus the police, prosecutors, and laws need to be tougher on sex offenders. The privileging of stories about golden girls being stolen by evil villains narrows the discussion of risk. If, as Maxwell

McCombs and Donald Shaw have argued, the media cannot tell people what to think but can tell them what to think *about*, then treating only certain kinds of murders as events causes a great deal of harm. The reasons these narratives offer for the risks that girls and women face—while terrifying and tragic—are actually comforting in comparison to stories of imperfect families of all classes, of poverty, or of violence that are more representative of the dangers facing citizens.

A discussion of these systematic harms lacks the horrifying but compelling lyricisim of golden girls lost. Such discussions involve statistics, violence so repetitive as to become mundane, and a call for action that cannot easily be addressed through focusing on one kind of risk or single bad actors. An examination of the kinds of stories told about two missing girls, Natalee Holloway and LaToyia Figueroa, demonstrates how complex stories about multiple risk factors lose out to simple stories about golden white innocence. The gendered unmaking of LaToyia Figueroa illustrates why missing women of color and men do not become national events and signs of a nation's grief, and it also suggests the ethical costs when certain citizens continually occupy nonevent status. In the cultural logic of abduction stories, "complexity" means mystery, not attention to the multifaceted risks threatening women, children, and men. Such exclusivity in event making thus poses risks for all citizens whose complex stories are effaced in favor of the comfort offered by the Lost Girl Event.

The story of Natalee Holloway's disappearance became a significant Lost (White) Girl Event not only because of the massive media coverage but because it was the Lost Girl Event that ushered in, in 2005, the media's most prominent self-reflexive attention to its own attachments to these kinds of stories. As Eugene Robinson writes, these "damsel in distress" stories are "meta-narratives" about "something seen as precious and delicate being snatched away, defiled, destroyed by evil forces that lurk in the shadows, just outside the bedroom window. It's whiteness under siege. It's innocence and optimism crushed by cruel reality. It's a flower smashed by a rock" ("Cable" A19). In the early hours of May 30, 2005, eighteen-year-old Natalee Holloway disappeared in Aruba while on a senior class trip. Holloway's disappearance was featured almost every day on the cable news channels for weeks. As I write this, the prime suspect has not been charged, and Holloway remains missing. Holloway was repeatedly described as beautiful, and media commentators discussed her future plans to be a doctor—all descriptors that served a national event narrative about an innocent girl with a golden future.

The importance of mothers in constructions of innocence is apparent in Holloway's case. Abductions of young adult women are often narrated in relation to their status as someone's child, a habitual framing mechanism for telling stories about injury and loss in the United States— lost men, in fact, are more likely be legible when they are soldiers whose mothers grieve their loss.[7] In one episode of *Nancy Grace*, a commentator from *America's Most Wanted* stated that Holloway's mother, Beth Twitty, "personifies the ultimate crusading mother," "somebody who refuses to walk away quietly," is "always available to do interviews," and "does all the right things." Twitty made a plea to other parents when she asked for support to keep two of the suspects from leaving Aruba: "I am asking all mothers and fathers in all nations to hear my plea" ("Mothers"). The story of child abduction is thus not only a story of those who are legally children; it is the story of those who are presented in the press as someone's child. Parents are obviously best situated to present the missing as perpetually innocent; adult women who are lost are, to their mothers and fathers, baby girls. The role of parents is yet another example of how time is fragmented in the event narrative: the woman is also child, and thus adult women can be made into Lost Girl Events.

The innocence requirement of Lost Girl Events is explicit in the discourse of the Carole Sund/Carrington Memorial Foundation, an organization devoted to bringing attention to the missing and murdered and pursuing justice for them and their families. The foundation is key to helping promote the Holloway case and other high-profile abductions (Burrough). It offers rewards for information about people who are missing, and the first criterion in the list of factors that must be present for financial help is innocence: "All victims must be innocent; must not engage in illegal activity" (Carole). This may be a simple way of reducing the number of requests for help: the foundation does not offer rewards to return children who are kidnapped by one of their parents, a much more common kind of abduction than stranger abduction. The foundation seems to be focusing on the kind of rare, random crime that befell Carole Sund, her daughter, and friend—a random attack by a stranger that is typically harder to solve than the more frequent crimes committed by someone known to the victim. Nevertheless, the phrasing is striking: as opposed to stating simply that people who were committing crimes when they were abducted are not eligible for help, the foundation prefaces that stricture with the "innocence" proviso. Despite the clarification about illegal activity that follows the initial phrase, the words "all victims must be innocent" seem to have a larger scope than mere illegality; otherwise, the stricture against illegal activity would have been sufficient.

The institutional validation of innocence results in a perversion of the traditional idea of utilitarianism that I see as a kind of fairy-tale utilitarianism—supporting the greatest good for the greatest *good* number. Individuals, lost in utilitarianism, are lost here too, as the individual comes to stand for the abstract child and her family. Fairy-tale utilitarianism supports the prevention of harm to those who are constructed as ideal citizens, who do nothing that might place them at risk for harm. The innocence rule does not suggest that some people deserve their harm, but it does gesture to the idea of responsibility in relationship to crimes that befall citizens. The innocence proviso also gestures toward the reality that there is typically more urgency attached to finding the "innocent" and those viewed as "innocent" than to locating those who are more likely to be harmed because of their own activities such as drug use. The questionable rationale for this privileging of the "innocent" reveals affective cultural priorities. The first is that because people engaged in illegal acts (which could include something as common as underage drinking) are more likely to be harmed, it is less of a mystery when they are injured; their victimization poses less of a threat to the greater population. However, those that the Lost Girl Event characterizes as "not innocent" constitute a greater number of the disappeared and murdered, which suggests that these victims need even greater protection in order to prevent more deaths. In terms of number of victims and of investigative importance, reason would dictate that a coalition of media and advocates for the lost not naturalize attentiveness to idealized citizens.

In response to a defense attorney's suggestion that Holloway might have wandered off after drinking and drowned, a news commentator on the *Nancy Grace* show exclaimed, "This was a golden girl! She was in Bible study!" While the more persuasive rebuttal to this suggestion, which she later makes, is that one of the suspects changed his story, "golden girl" logic is powerful in the United States. Holloway has functioned as both an exceptional golden girl and as a representative of every "parent's worst nightmare" (Robinson, "Cable" A19). The construction of Holloway's representativeness—*and* that of her parents—elides differences between parents as well as tightening the parameters of what might produce every parent's worst nightmare. While the events that surround Holloway's disappearance and probable death remain unclear and may always remain so, the possibility that a heavy amount of alcohol consumption might have heightened her risk for harm makes her *more* representative of every parent's worst nightmare and not less. As alcohol plays a role in the death, sexual assault, and injury of many teenagers, a story about Holloway that leaves room for the possibility of irresponsible alcohol consumption could make the event of Holloway's disappearance a more representative one—particularly if the event was narrated in a way that refrained from judgmentally dismissing her disappearance because she might have taken more precautions with her safety.

The erasure of the possible role of alcohol in Holloway's disappearance is only one example of how representativeness is crafted elliptically. While stranger abductions represent only 3 percent of missing children a year, these stories have been constructed as a pressing issue facing contemporary U.S. families (NISMART 2). The privileging of golden girl stories depends upon the erasure of widespread harms. For example, in the decades bracketing the turn of the twenty-first century, the murders of boys were far less likely to receive national attention. That lack of attention is not because girls are more likely to be murdered. At least 24,950 children were murdered between 1980 and 2000; 77 percent of them were male, and they were disproportionately of color (U.S. Department of Justice). While the names of girls fill the media when they are abducted or assaulted, boys are not similarly constructed as vulnerable unless attacks on their bodies can be narrated in relation to anxieties about homosexuality.[8] Much of the violence occurring between juveniles facilitates the ideological construction of boys—particularly black and brown boys—as something other than innocent victims. The erasure of boys and other children who do not fit the paradigm of the golden girl signals more than neglect; their absence is as important as the privileging of the golden girl child. The difference between idealized victims and others demonstrates which discourses make victims legible to the state or media. As Patricia Williams points out in her discussion of a Supreme Court case that determined that states can "choose whether or not [they] will protect children from abuse," protective legislation is overdetermined by short-term (and yet, deeply ideologically entrenched) cultural desires.[9] "What," Williams asks, "would a child have to introduce as currency by which care of the state would be made a right?"(35). The currency of innocence means that the massive coverage of the Holloway disappearance is defended on the grounds that it represents "every parent's nightmare," while the disappearance of the pregnant, twenty-four-year-old black Latina LaToyia Figueroa received coverage only because it would be constructed as "'every black and/or Latino parent's nightmare'" (Robinson, "Cable" A19).

The disappearance of LaToyia Figueroa and how it was constructed, by turns as a "black" story or an "American" one, illustrates how the Other defines what Deleuze describes as the "perceptual field" of the event (307). We could not understand the privileging of Natalee Holloway without the devaluing of other kinds of citizens as nongolden. "The *a priori* Other, as the absolute structure" makes the structure of the fairy tale (307). Without LaToyias, unnamed and ignored *or* named and vilified, there could be not be Natalees. The story of the discourse circulating around Figueroa's disappearance calls attention not only to the challenge of mobilizing affect for those who fall outside of Lost Girl narratives but to the challenge of addressing stories of the missing and murdered that are "not a mystery" and thus not an "event," as are the majority of such disappearances. People are more likely to be assaulted by their loved ones than by anyone else. How do we sell stories that do not seem to be news because they refer to systematic harms?

LaToyia Figueroa's disappearance in Philadelphia was initially a mystery. On July 18, 2005, the pregnant Figueroa went to her doctor's office with the father of the baby she was carrying but then failed to pick up her seven-year-old daughter at day care later that day. Figueroa's family had already lived through at least one violent death—LaToyia's mother had been murdered in 1985 at the age of twenty-two (Weichselbaum). A month later, she was found strangled; the police were led to her body by the father of her unborn child. He was subsequently arrested and convicted of her murder. She was partially identified by the angel tattooed on her wrist, a tragic and ironic marker of the distance between the cultural constructions of black single mothers and idealized white girls (Memmott 3A).

Disappearing approximately six week after Holloway, Figueroa became, like Alexis Patterson, a story worthy of national attention because it was seen as revealing a possible news bias. Blogger Richard Blair called attention to Figueroa's disappearance. Blair, as *Philadelphia Magazine* columnist Noel Weyrich suggested, "shamed" the national networks into covering the story. But Weyrich argues that Blair's "throwing down the race card" ignores the fact that many women of all races disappear and "don't get the Natalee Holloway treatment on CNN" because "the details are too depressing. Many involve women who hook up with bad men in bad circumstances and come to a bad end. It's sad. It's tragic. It's not news." For Weyrich, Holloway's disappearance was news, possessing "that stranger-than-fiction quality" that supposedly defines a media event. Strange, in Weyrich's analysis, also means innocent. Figueroa's identity, as the often vilified unwed black single mother, makes her into something other than female. Single black motherhood makes her into something Other, otherness mobilized by the politics of disgust that undergirds discourse about poorer black women in the United States.[10] Weyrich argues that "if there is any chance her poor judgment or bad behavior helped seal her fate," the victim will not receive attention. The high-profile murder of pregnant Laci Peterson by her husband Scott received attention, Weyrich argues, because

> *she was a sweet and trusting expectant mother, preparing to live out the American Dream with a handsome responsible husband—who just happened to be a homicidal sociopath. Laci's story was Hollywood. LaToyia's story—unmarried, scratching out a living, knocked up by some lowlife probationer, isn't.*

Weyrich is right to argue that "media coverage of the missing and murdered is not about fairness or responsible news standards—it's about myths and fables, the perfect husband with a secret, the dark side of an island paradise, the evil that lurks within." However, in making his claim to being "realistic" about media coverage, he fails to address three other "realities." First, it is untrue to suggest that we cannot and should not hold the media responsible for fairness and responsible news standards. This would not necessarily entail blanketing the airwaves with reports on the disappearances of everyone, which is not feasible, but it *would* involve covering a diverse set of stories that would allow the media to bring all of their storytelling skills to bear upon an incident in order to make it an event. Weyrich also argues that "facts" kill a story faster than anything else, but he ignores the capacity of the news to set agendas. Second, the issue of bad judgment is a significant one in the American imaginary, but as any number of Lifetime movies for women demonstrate, a story about a woman's bad judgment often finds a market. This claim relates to his third point, the disingenuous statement that the inequity in coverage is not about race at all. Yet, although a disproportionate percentage of the missing are people of color, *none* of them receive the attention directed to the disappearances of Laci Peterson, Natalee Holloway, or Elizabeth Smart. While it is true that many white women go missing and remain largely anonymous beyond their communities, it is clearly significant that many of the missing are people of color and that they do not get national attention—with two notable exceptions that I will discuss—because race *is* a factor. Any number of people could fit into the innocence proviso. It is clear that race, class, and gender have an effect. Weyrich's last criterion—sensationalism—is a more complicated one. However, the high-profile story of Laci Peterson, a woman killed by her husband, who did not even have a documented record of being a batterer, is not a new kind of story. Events are not sensational in themselves; they are made into sensations. Weyrich naturalizes the process by which these stories become news, but we cannot forget that there are mechanisms for circulating stories and mobilizing affect on behalf of victims.

LaToyia Figueroa's story was briefly made into an event—albeit only in relationship to a Lost White Girl. How do advocates for the lost black girl make a Lost Black Girl Event? The answer in Figueroa's case was a combination of guilt and shame—two affects that have been used successfully to counter apathy in u.s. culture. These affects also came into play in stories about two lost African American girls, Sherrice Iverson and Rilya Wilson. These lost girls were two of the few bodies of color whose names were mapped onto law. However, the laws shaped by their victimization lacked national support. The legacy that might have spawned from their deaths vanished, like the stories of their victimization, into ghost stories about a local tragedy. Iverson's and Wilson's stories demonstrate how and why the bodies of people of color circulate on a national scale, but they also remind us that there are mechanisms for making certain kinds of sympathy national policy. Far from being a natural process, event making takes political framing. From the Birmingham Church bombing to the Rodney King beating and ensuing l.a. riots, transforming harm to oppressed bodies into national events has been important in framing the immediacy of social justice concerns.[11]

I Do Not Know This Little Girl

Instead of trying to prevent event making, we should recognize that it is an inevitable media practice and sometimes an ethical one. Ethical event making in the u.s. media involves understanding the possibilities of the world as defined by others. Negotiating what Deleuze calls the a priori Other, that which defines the possibilities available to us as subjects, and the *concrete* other, real bodies that articulate entirely other worlds, is critical. I would reframe this account in terms of the tension between abstract and specific other bodies, between those that are not featured in fairy-tale fictions and the bodies that challenge the ethical logic of privileging certain citizens when the costs of devaluing other lives is made explicit. It is the difference between Elizabeth and Alexis, between privileging missing white children whose status depends upon the shadow of other bodies and the proactive disregard of injured black girls. Negotiating the difference between the abstract and the real also involves recognizing the balance between threats to all citizens and those that more frequently threaten less advantaged citizens. U.S. child protection must negotiate this divide, treating events that are both universal and specific.

Events that become law are profound examples of the political implications of bodies becoming events. Mapping names of victims onto law, as in the case of Megan's Law, is a fairly new phenomenon. Memorial laws are named after crime victims, and it is a phenomenon that became more common in the 1990s.[12] There are two bodies wrapped into a piece of crime legislation named for victims: the first is the victim and the second is the kind of person who committed the crime. Memorial legislation is perhaps the most concrete manifestation of the temporal fragmentation of event; its thrust is what has happened and what might happen.[13] The two most well-known pieces of memorial legislation carry the names of child victims, Megan's Law and the Ambler Alert system, both laws designed to protect future victims. Named after Amber Hagerman, who was abducted and murdered in 1996, the Amber Alert is a system that notifies a community when a child is missing in ways similar to notification about weather emergencies. These murdered girls became signs of the possible future of other girls like them if the state fails to act.

In contrast, temporal anxiety has not propelled the prominent nationalization of memorial legislation about children of color. If memorial legislation is about "our" children's futures, black children, whose material circumstances often thwart their futures, are sometimes left out of the "our" of child protection. This nationalization of child protection legislation did not occur after laws were created for two high-profile African American girl victims. And yet these cases are instructive as examples of the victimization of children of color *temporarily* becoming national events. In 1997, a seven-year-old African American child named Sherrice Iverson was raped and murdered in the bathroom of a casino. The loss of her life could have been averted if a college student named David Cash, who saw the crime being committed by his best friend, had chosen to report it. This case prompted the Sherrice Iverson Child Victim Protection Act in the year 2000, or the "Good Samaritan Law," requiring people to report a violent or sexual assault of a child to the police. Some believe the law does not do enough; others believe that it is a problematic and reactionary response to a terrible crime.[14] But in a decade of legislation named after victims, it was the first piece of crime legislation to be named for an African American.

The lesson to be learned from this case, however, lies with why Sherrice's tragic, preventable story incited outrage that produced legislation. A hint at the challenge for those working on behalf of those marked with normalized suffering is revealed by the "bad samaritan's" words. In an effort to explain his failure to act in response to the attack on Iverson, Cash said, "I do not know this little girl. I do not know starving children in Panama. I do not know people who die of disease in Egypt" (Gorov). His callous words highlight the ways in which political action is often predicated on valuing victims who are similar to ourselves or those we love, and that the absence of identification often produces inaction. While some might clinically mark Cash as a sociopath, he nonetheless demonstrates the political challenge of cultivating compassion for those marked as other. His apathy, interfering dramatically with the narratives many u.s. citizens might tell about their capacity for compassion, made Sherrice Iverson's death a national event. Unlike high-profile white girls, her incorporealization is not defined by verbs such as murdered, abducted, or raped, but by the fact that she was ignored. Philosophers and political theorists have long discussed the ways in which sympathy, compassion, or pity play a role in the maintenance of the state. But the example of Cash invites the question: how can the state mandate compassion? He makes Sherrice Iverson's suffering foreign and alien, implying that it is logical for him to feel no compassion for "foreign" brown bodies. For Cash, Iverson is not and could not possibly be part of his family. His radical indifference highlights the necessity of producing a rhetoric that makes the attack on "other" children an attack on the home, that reminds those who witness suffering that systemic victimization indicts a society that fails to express outrage. Instead of making the sensational the everyday, advocates for the less visible must make the everyday sensational.

While the devaluing of certain kinds of victims is everyday, the Iverson case was not. If one of the problems with Megan's Law is that it makes an infrequent harm representative, the same might be said for the Iverson bill. Cash seems atypical in his unapologetic monstrosity. u.s. citizens rarely admit to the press that they feel apathy for what happens to children. What is interesting about the bill is that it arose in response to outrage that he could so unapologetically devalue Iverson, and few want to suggest that u.s. citizens devalue some children. Certainly the idea of a devalued class of citizen emerged as a narrative with Rilya Wilson, an African American girl who disappeared and garnered media attention. But as opposed to the Iverson Act, there are a great number of arguments to be made for why the Rilya Wilson Act is a piece of legislation that should have spread beyond the state of Florida.

In 2002, the Department of Children and Families (DCF) in Florida was embroiled in a highly public scandal because of a missing girl named Rilya Wilson. Wilson had been placed in foster care by the DCF, which had removed her from her mother because of a substance abuse problem. Caseworkers were obligated to see Rilya every month, but it was over a year before the agency realized that she was missing. Rilya Wilson was four years old at the time of her disappearance. Her caregiver, allegedly her paternal grandmother, said that a representative from the DCF had taken her away for tests in January 2001 and that she had never seen her again. Eventually, Rilya's caregiver was arrested for her murder, but as I write this, her body has still not been found.

Simply the facts of this case, delivered without frills, are sensational. The tragedy can be summarized by a phrase often repeated in this story—"no one noticed" that a four-year-old under the care of the state was missing. False reports were submitted, indicating that a caseworker had been seeing the child. Stories of Florida's DCF losing children filled the national media. In many ways, Rilya Wilson serves as the most prominent signifier of the nonevent status of some children's lives, while also demonstrating that the media and citizens *can* become invested in children who do not fit the profile of the Lost White Girl. While high-profile Lost White Girls have parents to mobilize affect for them, it was the media that took up the role of championing Wilson. Governor Jeb Bush signed the Rilya Wilson Act, which requires children age three and above who are under state supervision to attend a day care program or school five days a week. Any unexcused absences must be promptly reported to the agency responsible for their care.

Wilson's story fell out of the limelight. Florida papers did continue to remember her story and discuss the dysfunction at the DCF, but there were few reports in the national media about her caregiver's arrest.[15] Nor has there been a *sustained* high-profile national discussion about the issues that Rilya's case brings to the fore. The absence of Rilya Wilson's story, as opposed to the continued presence of stranger abduction narratives about individual children lost to sexual predators, brings up issues that affect a very large number of children in the United States. Moreover, to tell Wilson's story, with all its complexities, is to tell a story about the struggles of many U.S. citizens, not only of children.

To tell a story about Rilya Wilson is to tell a story about children in foster care, what brought them there, and the risks to their lives. In 2002, the year Rilya was reported missing, over half a million children were in foster care (Children's Defense Fund). These children are more likely to experience poverty, substance abuse, and mental health problems than other children. They are overwhelmingly placed in foster care because of potential neglect or abuse—and in 2002 over 900,000 reports of abuse were confirmed by agencies across the country, a number that is generally considered to underestimate the number of victimized children. Of these children, 1,500 died from maltreatment (Children's). Even if this number also includes the murders resulting from stranger abductions, a far greater number of children die because of a complex set of systemic harms rather than in highly publicized kidnapping cases.

To talk about foster care children is to produce more complex stories about danger and the things that place children at risk for foster care—namely poverty and substance abuse (Children's). While the vast majority of the poor do not abuse their children, the inability to make a living wage and the seductions of drugs in a world offering few chances for transforming lives can heighten the risks for abuse. As the Children's Defense Fund argues, not recognizing that the dangers to children are often a result of the dangers to *families*, a result of the erosion of economic justice, is to ignore what children really need in order to survive and thrive in U.S. culture.

Rilya Wilson's story is complex and therefore harder to tell or sell. The evils are more diffuse and would demand an attack on forces that cannot be easily defined as aberrant others preying on youth. The Rilya Wilson Act asks for the bare minimum of attention: simply that children be *noticed*. While some may have found it easy to construct a version of the simple story—a bad black caregiver, an incompetent state worker—such simple stories do not really address the greater dangers confronting the nation. If the stories of missing and murdered children in the United States allow for the mapping of lost bodies onto national anxieties about dangers to America, then the dangers facing Rilya, other foster children, their families, and all citizens should loom large as omnipresent monsters to fight. While some suggest that the loss of children and women like Alexis,

LaToyia, or Rilya is inevitable, given their circumstances, and thus less newsworthy, activists must resist the naturalization of national concern and sympathy. For a brief moment, citizens were haunted by Rilya's loss, but she had no parent or group to continue to agitate for her and others like her. Advocates for those like Rilya must make her loss an event, still utilizing and revising the story of the lost individual to call attention to structural evils but eschewing the temptation to privilege evils that are individualized and easy to lock away.

My argument here is *not* that we should stop caring about lost white girls and women, or even that such disappearances should never become events. But the nationalization and naturalization of some events have costs. The focus on missing white girls as an inevitable product of market and public interest ignores the fact that such event making is an orchestrated political practice and not an inescapable and inalterable product of cultural desires or capitalist investments. Imagining event making as an ethical practice, one in which those categorized as others would be privileged, can allow us to see the transformative possibilities of making not only lost girls but the loss of other kinds of bodies into events. We must fight to privilege tales about structural kinds of evils, tales that tell of more elaborate events and of monsters that are more diffuse and harder to fight. In its own, odd way, the horrifying story of Natalee Holloway, which is "every parent's worse nightmare," provides more ideological comfort to the nation than stories of the everyday terrors that afflict most citizens. When we successfully nationalize everyday events, all lost citizens, and not only a few lost girls, will be safer.

Notes

I thank Lloyd Pratt, Kevin Haynes, Evie Shockley, Lu Zhang, and the editors at *differences* for their help with this essay.

REBECCA WANZO is Assistant Professor of Women's Studies and African American and African Studies at the Ohio State University. She is currently completing a book manuscript about sentimental political storytelling in the United States forthcoming from SUNY Press.

1   JonBenét Ramsey was a six-year-old girl found murdered in her parents' basement the day after Christmas in 1996. The news coverage focused extensively on her participation in beauty pageants for young girls. Laci Peterson was a pregnant woman who disappeared in 2002. She was later found murdered. Her husband was eventually convicted of the crime. I discuss Elizabeth Smart, Megan Kanka, and Natalee Holloway later in this essay. The Lani Guinier and Gerald Torres quotation in the epigraph is from *The Miner's Canary* 11.

2   See Children's Defense Fund
     and National Adolescent Health
     Information Center.

3   See also Edelman, whose psy-
     choanalytic reading of the child's
     centrality to political discourse
     argues that queer bodies are a
     threat to this kind of citizen-
     ship discourse because of their
     distance from reproduction.
     His articulation of the child as
     "inner child" might also provide
     an interesting slant on what the
     child body actually represents
     for the white, adult, middle-class
     citizen that is allegedly the object
     of the Lost Girl Event.

4   For a history of the Atlanta Child
     Murders, see Detlinger and Pugh;
     and Headley.

5   Kanka's mother testified that "at
     first she wasn't unduly concerned
     when she didn't see her daughter
     because 'this is such a nice
     neighborhood.'" See Burney.

6   Jennifer Carol Wilbanks ran away
     a few days before her wedding in
     April 2005, and her disappear-
     ance spawned a national search.
     A few days later she called from
     a hotel room and falsely claimed
     that she had been abducted. She
     was dubbed the "Runaway Bride."

7   Such language is reminiscent of
     the nineteenth-century rhetoric
     that appealed to maternal empa-
     thy. See Cappuccio; and *Nancy
     Grace*, "Mothers."

8   An obvious example of the focus
     on boys was the child sexual
     abuse scandal that rocked the
     Catholic Church in 2002. For
     more on this, see Clark.

9   In *DeShaney v. Winnebago County
     Department of Social Services*

(1989), it was ruled that the state
does not have a constitutional
duty to protect citizens from harm
by a third party.

10   For more on the politics of
     disgust, see Hancock.

11   There has been a great deal of
     scholarship on the importance of
     certain events to framing black
     political rhetoric in the United
     States. See Fiske; and Jacobs.
     On the civil rights movement,
     see Torres. On Emmett Till, see
     Spratt et al. On the civil rights
     movement and the way that
     events shape collective memory,
     see Harris.

12   Even the National Center for the
     Victims of Crime cannot accu-
     rately tabulate how many pieces
     of legislation have memorialized
     victims, but one journalist esti-
     mates that between January 2003
     and June 2004, over fifty pieces
     of legislation named for victims
     were passed. See Russakoff.

13   One of the first pieces of legisla-
     tion named for victims in the late
     twentieth century that gained
     widespread coverage was the
     Brady Bill, a federal piece of leg-
     islation that required a five-day
     waiting period and background
     check for gun purchases. Named
     for James Brady, who was shot
     in an attempted assassination
     of Ronald Regan in 1981, it was
     signed into law in 1993.

14   For a critique of the Iverson Act,
     see Vance.

15   *The St. Petersburg Times* contin-
     ued to cover the trial against her
     caregiver and issues at Florida's
     DCF.

Works Cited   Benson, Lee. "We Pray We Find an Angel." *Deseret News* 7 June 2002: B1.

Berlant, Lauren. *The Queen of America Goes to Washington City: Essays on Sex and Citizenship.* Durham: Duke UP, 1997.

Blair, Richard. "Missing Non-white Woman Alert!" *All Spin Zone: Progressive Politics Writ Large.* 22 July 2005. http://allspinzone.com/wp/2005/07/page/7/.

Burney, Melanie. "Trial Begins of Neighbor Charged in Death of 'Megan's Law' Girl." *Associated Press* 5 May 1997.

Burrough, Bryan. "Missing White Female." *Vanity Fair* Jan. 2006. LexisNexis 2 Dec. 2007. http://lexisnexis.com.

Cappuccio, Nicole. "Mother of Soldiers and the Iraq War: Justification through Breakfast Shows on ABC, CBS, and NBC." *Women and Language* 29.1 (2006): 3–9.

Carole Sund/Carrington Memorial Foundation. "Services Available." http://www.carolesund foundation.com/sections/about/services.

Children's Defense Fund. "The State of America's Children 2005." Children's Defense Fund. 9 Apr. 2007. http://campaign.childrensdefense.org/publications/greenbook/default.aspx.

Clark, Stephen. "Gay Priests and Other Bogeymen." *Journal of Homosexuality* 51 (2006): 1–13.

Deleuze, Gilles. *The Logic of Sense.* 1969. Ed. Constantin V. Boundas. Trans. Mark Lester with Charles Stivale. New York: Columbia UP, 1990.

DeShaney v. Winnebago County Department of Social Services. 489 U.S. 189. U.S. Sup. Ct. 1989.

Dettlinger, Chet, and Jeff Prugh. *The List.* Atlanta: Philmay Enterprises, 1984.

Dougherty, Kerry. "Beauty and Wealth Drive Coverage of Kidnapping." *Virginian-Pilot* 20 June 2002: B6.

Ecols, Mike. *I Know My First Name Is Steven.* New York: Pinnacle, 1999.

Edelman, Lee. *No Future: Queer Theory and the Death Drive.* Durham: Duke UP, 2004.

Entman, Robert M., and Andrew Rojecki. *The Black Image in the White Mind: Media and Race in America* (2000). Chicago: U of Chicago P, 2001.

Fass, Paula S. *Kidnapped: Child Abduction in America.* New York: Oxford UP, 1997.

Fiske, John. *Media Matters: Everyday Culture and Political Change.* Minneapolis: U of Minnesota P, 1994.

Glassner, Barry. *The Culture of Fear: Why Americans Are Afraid of the Wrong Things.* New York: Basic Books, 2000.

Gorov, Linda. "Outrage Follows Cold Reply to Killing." *Boston Globe* 7 Aug. 1998: A1.

Guinier, Lani, and Gerald Torres. *The Miner's Canary: Enlisting Race, Resisting Power, Transforming Democracy.* Cambridge: Harvard UP, 2002.

Hancock, Ange-Marie. *The Politics of Disgust: The Public Identity of the Welfare Queen.* New York: New York UP, 2004.

Harris, Frederick C. "It Takes a Tragedy to Arouse Them: Collective Memory and Collective Action during the Civil Rights Movement." *Social Movement Studies* 5.1 (2006): 19–43.

Headley, Bernard. *The Atlanta Child Murders and the Politics of Race*. Carbondale: Southern Illinois UP, 1999.

Jacobs, Ronald N. *Race, Media, and the Crisis of Civil Society: From Watts to Rodney King*. New York: Cambridge UP, 2000.

Jerome, Richard, and Maria Eftimiades. "Megan's Legacy." *People* 43.11 (1995): 46–51. EBSCO 13 Nov. 2007. http://web.ebscohost.com.

Jurkowitz, Mark. "The Media: Two Missing Girls, but Only One Big Story / Some See Race, Class Affecting Coverage." *Boston Globe* 19 June 2002: D1.

Lutton, Christine. "Promise of Puppy Lured Her to Death." *Philadelphia Inquirer* 2 Aug. 1994: A6.

McCombs, Maxwell, and Donald Shaw. "The Agenda Setting Function of the Mass Media." *Public Opinion Quarterly* 36.2 (1972): 176–87.

Memmott, Mark. "Missing Pregnant Woman Found Dead." *USA Today* 22 Aug. 2005: 3A.

Mike. "Help LaToyia Figueroa." Online posting. 29 July 2005. *SkaroffBlog*. http://skaroff .com/blog/index.php/2005/07/29/help-latoyia-figueroa/.

Moran, Terry. "The Market for Murder: Why True-Life Tales of Terror Warm Our Hearts." *Washington Post* 10 Aug. 1997: C1.

Mothers against Predators. MothersAgainstPredators.org. http://www.mothersagainst predators.org/.

Nancy Grace. CNN Headline News 5 June 2005. www.cnn.com/CNN/Programs/nancy/ grace.

—————————-. "Mothers of Missing Children Speak Out." CNNHN 12 May 2006.

National Adolescent Health Information Center. "Fact Sheet on Mortality: Adolescents and Young Adults." San Francisco: National Adolescent Health Information Center, University of California, San Francisco, 2000.

NISMART 2 U.S. Department of Justice (National Incidence Study of Missing, Abducted, Runaway, and Throwaway Children). Oct. 2002. www.cybertipline.com/en_us/documents/ nismart2_overview.pdf.

"On Barbara Lee Drive Could Megan Kanka's Life Have Been Saved if Her Parents Knew More about Their Neighbors?" Editorial. *Philadelphia Inquirer* 3 Aug. 1994: A10.

Quindlen, Anna. "The Passion to Keep Them Safe." *New York Times* 6 Aug. 1994: 19.

Robinson, Eugene. "Cable Can't Get beyond the Pale." *Washington Post* 12 Aug. 2005: A19.

—————————. "(White) Women We Love." *Washington Post* 10 June 2005: A23.

Russakoff, Dale. "Out of Grief Comes a Legislative Force." *Washington Post* 15 June 1998: A10.

Spillers, Hortense. "Mama's Baby, Papa's Maybe: An American Grammar Book." *Culture and Countermemory: The "American" Connection*. Spec. issue of *Diacritics* 17.2 (1987): 64–81.

Spratt, Margaret, Cathy Ferrance Bullock, Gerald Baldasty, et al. "News, Race, and the Status Quo: The Case of Emmett Till." *Howard Journal of Communication* 18.2 (Apr. 2007): 169–92.

Torres, Sasha. "'In a Crisis We Must Have a Sense of Drama': Civil Rights and Televisual Information." *Channeling Blackness: Studies on Television and Race in America*. Ed. Darnell M. Hunt. New York: Oxford UP, 2005.

U.S. Department of Justice. *Juvenile Justice Bulletin*. Sept. 2004. "Trends in the Murder of Juveniles: 1980–2000." http://www.ojp.usdoj.gov./ojjdp.

Vance, Natalie Perrin-Smith. "My Brother's Keeper? The Criminalization of Nonfeasance: A Constitutional Analysis of Duty to Report Statutes." *California Western Law Review* 36 (Fall 1999): 135–55.

Wald, Priscilla. *Constituting Americans: Cultural Anxiety and Narrative Form*. Durham: Duke UP, 1994.

Waxman, Sharon. "Salt Lake Kidnapping Spurs Wide Search: Police Have Few Leads on Who Took Girl, 14, from Home at Gunpoint." *Washington Post* 7 June 2002: A3.

Weichselbaum, Simone. "Friends Fear Missing Woman May Share Her Mother's Tragic Fate." *Philadelphia Daily News* 30 July 2005. LexisNexis 6 Apr. 2007. http://lexisnexis.com.

Weyrich, Noel. "Contrarian: Attack of the Blogs!" *Philadelphia Magazine* Oct. 2005. http://www.phillymag.com/home/articles/contrarian_attack_ of_the_blogs/.

Williams, Patricia. *The Alchemy of Race and Rights*. Cambridge: Harvard UP, 1991.

Aftereffects of the End of the World ("I ♥ NY")

*T*he end is near, in some ways always. Near because the end marks the close or termination of that which is here now, that which will have been an event when it passes. The proximity of an end determines the event: the event takes place, comes to be seen as an event in its end, as the event of the end as much as the end of an event. (The event is determined by the proximity of the end, its nearness, as much as by the end itself: the event of nearness and the nearness of the event.) Yet suspended in the grammar of the event is the status of the article that ends it: *an* end or *the* end? One end among many possible ends or means, or the end, an absolute limit against which everything ends and beyond which nothing is possible?

According to a logic of the event extended by Jacques Derrida, what separates the event from a performative act, from that which makes something happen, from that which makes something arrive in its performance, is its singularity and unpredictability: the event is never anticipated or intended and can never be repeated. A speech act, and especially a performative speech act, operates according to the condition of

Volume 19, Number 2   DOI 10.1215/10407391-2008-006

repeatability and of predictability that allows one to anticipate an action on the occasion of an utterance. Each such act takes place already as a form of repetition in advance, even if it occurs only once. (Its repetition is inscribed in the possibility of each speech act.) By contrast, there is no language of the event in advance, no idiom, and no possibility of repetition. It arrives suddenly without iteration or iterability. "One of the characteristics of the event," says Derrida, "is that not only does it come about as something unforeseeable, not only does it disrupt the ordinary course of history, but it is also absolutely singular" ("Certain" 223). Unforeseen and irreproducible, the event as well as its end are established in this singularity—the end as much as the event. Not any end, not one of any number of possible ends. This end, the end.

By virtue of its singularity, this end—the end—ends this event and all others. The end of the event is the end as such; and the event as such and its end are in themselves events. A finite circularity dictates the logic of the end and of the event and of the interpenetration of the two: the end is an event and the event an end. Each in relation to the other determines a finitude that is nonetheless circular and deferred, immediate and postponed. That is, the event and the end always arrive in the present, now. The absence of predictability and iterability confine the event to the present, but a present not given (in its entirety) to the present. The event of the end signals the end of the present, of presence, in the present. If the structure of the end as event is singular in its appearance and thus finite, is any end anything less than the end of not only one event but of every event, of everything, including you, me, and the world? What then of the end of the event and its chiasmic trace, the event of the end? What takes place in the end, as the end, as the event of the end, in this crossing of the two? Is it the last event, the end of the event, of eventuality? Or the exemplary event, which comes to pass eventually, as the essence of all events?

What Kind of Event Is the End?

Every event is marked by a relation to the end, by an eventuality of the end that renders each event always an end in itself. What one calls an event is significant because of the end it signifies, the radical transformation it signals, the belief that in the wake of an event, everything changes. A different world emerges after the event. But the rhetoric of the end, like that of the origin, is itself commonplace, frequently invoked and threatened, in spite of the apocalyptic singularity it signals. (How many ends can come to pass before the end of all ends?) A certain banality, a form of ordinary, predictable, and fully anticipated, which is to say preinscribed and prescribed, written and rewritten finality figures the rhetoric of the end of each event. The end of an era, the end of history, the end of man: everything comes to an end, and is measured, in the end, by its ability to reach its end, the end proper to it.

But even "the end of history" is not without a remainder; the human animal (or the animal remains of human being) comes at the end of history, along with happiness, or at least contentedness, according to Alexandre Kojève.[1] The end of history leaves everything intact—art, music, play, and love—but without proper affect; contentment (nature) without happiness (philosophy), without proper affect, which is to say without the affect that belongs properly to art, music, play, and love, and which in turn allows each of these activities, each of those events to belong to history. Proper affects are replaced by improper ones (inauthentic, imposter), which are not, according to the lineage from Hegel that Kojève traces, the affects that drive human activity toward the construction of history. The distinction is crucial, since the world remains the same and yet everything has changed: from history to affect, philosophy to natural feeling, everything that remains does so in the form of a useless affect. All the rest is restless, the remainder a restlessness. (In this aftermath of the end of history, says Kojève, the human being has become animal but also American and Japanese, materialist and formalist—two national states of the posthuman animal. In a series of footnotes appended to later editions of his lectures, Kojève claims that the era of the human being ended with history; he gives two examples of posthistorical, and one might say posthuman, activity in the wake of history: the American pursuit of materialism and the empty formalism of Japanese culture.)[2] What remains are aftereffects of humanity, or *affects*: a series of posts after the end, in the ruins of the end, from posthistory to posthuman animality.

Because the event cannot be anticipated, because it cannot be called forth, when it does arrive, it arrives nameless. Its arrival signals the end, the event as the end of the event, at the end of history and at the end of language. There is nothing to call the event when it arrives. Without language, the event brings only affects, improper affects without signs, words, or names: affects from the end of history, from the secrecy of the event that yields no name. If the event and the end, its end, and the event of the end are subsumed by a discourse that is itself common (religious, journalistic, colloquial—"all good things come to an end"), then another form of crisis can be seen in the rhetorical and idiomatic registers that might be called cryptonymic. That is, the very name of the event and its end, one's ability to call the event by its name, its proper name, come to an end in the event of the end. (According to the logic of the end that precludes anticipation, one can never call forth or out an event.) What is hidden by the event of the end, in the event of the end, is its name, the one proper to it, the name of the event, as well as the entire event of language as such—not only the (singular) name of the event but the entirety of language from which the name would emerge. All language is lost along with the name in the arrival of the event. (In this sense, the event is also always the event of the end of language.) The name of the event disappears in the end of descriptive language, leaving in its wake a series of codes, a stream of symbols, numbers, and affects that transcribe the event without giving name to it: another event in place of the name of the event.

An event that initiates the millennium and the rhetoric of its end (of a perpetual end already arrived and still to come) and leaves its own designation deferred can be seen in the so-called 911 ("nine-eleven")—an event or sequence of events (a date and sequence of numbers) that "changed everything." (From what to what? For whom? For everyone everywhere?) A rare numerical event in the American idiom, named in code, as it were, for that whose naming is postponed; a numerical euphemism that delays the end, the arrival of the end, its finitude, deferring the naming of the event of the end. It also bears the homonymic and perhaps ironically mimicked numbers of the emergency call number, 911. It is a strangely Asian nomenclature, as if borrowed from another dialect. Numbers are frequently inscribed in lieu of descriptions to name historical events in East Asia, as if the date could serve as a name, however temporarily or provisionally, a numerical name in place of the name, a code in place of a historical idiom not yet available in and as language. In China, the May Fourth Movement (五四運動, literally the 54 movement), commemorating the nationalist mobilization of May 4, 1919; and its echo in the Tiananmen Square Massacre, known as the June Fourth Movement (六四運動, 64 movement), on June 4, 1989. In Korea, the Samil or 31 Movement (삼일 운동, 三一運動) against Japanese colonial rule on March 1, 1919. In Japan, the failed military coup d'état of February 26, 1936, known as the Niniroku Jiken (二二六事件, the 226 incident). In Taiwan, the 228 Incident (二二八事件) or slaughter of native Taiwanese by the Kuomintang (KMT) on February 28, 1947, and so on. (In each instance, the numbers are read separately as distinct digits and not as a composite number, "two two six" as opposed to "two hundred and twenty-six.") Significant historical events are designated by numerical codes extracted from dates: 54, 64, 31, 226, 228, 911. These events are unnamed, *described* by numbers, and reassigned numbers: designated, *designed*, designified. Numbers in place of words, a numeric code that signifies according to chains of meaning: 911 as the emergency call and the Madrid bombings of March 3, 2004 (known also as 311)—the discourse of terrorism—its provocation, which is also to say its pronunciation, rendered cryptonymically, *posted* as it were before the end and after it.[5]

"911 changed everything." 911 and not, for example, the event of slavery in America, itself an event without end, born of the endless refusal to acknowledge its eventness, an event without possible end perhaps, but one that still frames for D'nesh DeSouza an economy of the end when he mockingly refers to the history of slavery in the United States as "the end of racism." (For DeSouza, slavery in the United States, however racial, was never racist in nature; its end affirms for him the rejection of racism in the United States.) Everything changed with one event, here and everywhere, which is to say that no other event changed anything; or that no other event changed things as much as this one; or that this event establishes the event of events, the event that ends all other events, the event of the end itself, which came and is still always yet to come, to come to an end in the end of the event. "911 changed everything," an alarmist and opportunistic slogan exploited by the right, which follows from a series of catastrophic ends that haunts the last centuries of the last millennium, from North Atlantic slavery to the Shoah and Hiroshima and how many other massacres, rapes, crimes, disasters, and tragedies that define in euphemism the last century of the second millennium, the end of the last millennium, the millennium of ends? All things good and bad must come to an end, the platitudes of apocalypse and catastrophe, revelation and revolution (*katastrophē*, overturning).

The place of 911, its location in New York, on Wall Street at the heart of global capital, the last great metropolis of the old world (its end) and the first great city of the new world (its beginning) is significant in the figuring of 911 as that which changed everything. A liminal city between cultures, nations, and worlds, which on 911 is both Pearl Harbor and Hiroshima and 1,000 other sites of carnage unmapped on the psychic landscapes of American narcissism.[4] Sunil Bald, a New York-based architect and critic, notes the ways in which Hiroshima haunts the figure of Pearl Harbor in 911. In contrast to the post-911 responses to rebuilding the sites of the World Trade Center while preserving the survival of Manhattan itself, of "highlighting individual suffering within a city that hopes to remain fundamentally unchanged," Hiroshima, Bald says, "'forgets' its national tragedy by universalizing the event as a tragedy for humanity, a narrative that the city has been reconfigured to support" (54). In one scenario, the world is destroyed, but the universe—universality—preserved (Pearl Harbor, 911), while in the other, the end of the world is universalized (Hiroshima, 911). Pearl Harbor and Hiroshima erupt in 911, both are present in it in contradictory ways, but so is a history of unnamable events that remain suspended in or at the end of history, at the end of a series of historical breaks that marks the ruptures in or ends of history but not necessarily the end of history as such—between Pearl Harbor and Hiroshima, everything unnamed in between.

"I ♥ NY," "I Love New York." In the wake of the terrorist attacks, immediately heralded as an *event* (unforeseen, singular, transformative), the discourse turned to affect and identification, to a perverse form of displaced narcissism: universal sympathy. "Nous sommes tous Américains"; "Why do they hate us?"; "I ♥ NY MORE THAN EVER," the latter alluding to a publicity campaign for New York City from the 1970s. "I ♥ NY": Among the most visible iterations of the campaign was the T-shirt version, marketed to tourists as souvenirs and assumed in many cases by celebrity residents. (The T-shirt as such, named presumably for the shape it forms, can be traced to a military origin from World War I to World War II. The name also introduces a crypto-acronym: "T" is for . . . .) In this hybrid iteration, love is not a word but a symbol ♥ and following Peirce can be seen also as an index (from the body, an extension of and point of contact with it): the symbolic figure for love is placed on the location of the wearer's heart, forging a continuum between the body's inside and out, between depth and surface, between things and their representation, between organs and symbols. The ♥ emerges as an x-ray image of the organ; an inside brought to the surface and beyond, *exposed*. (A feature of the event is "exposure," says Derrida: "It is worth recalling that an event implies surprise, exposure, and the unanticipatable" ["Certain" 223].) An inside touches the outside and is touched in turn by that outside, moved, as it were, outside.

From *Wikipedia*, "I Love New York":

> *It is a famous pop-style icon that unabashedly promotes the metropolitan pride of New York State. In 1977, William S. Doyle, Deputy Commissioner of the New York State Department of*

Commerce hired advertising agency Wells Rich Greene to develop a marketing campaign for New York State. Doyle also recruited Milton Glaser, a productive graphic designer to work on the campaign, and he created the design based on Wells Rich Greene's advertising campaign. Glaser expected the campaign to last only a couple months and did the work pro bono. However, the design became a major success and has continued to be sold for years. The placement of the logo on plain white T-shirts readily sold in the city has widely circulated the appearance of the image, making it a commonly recognized symbol. The image became especially prominent following the September 11 terrorist attacks on the city, which created a sense of unity among the populace. Many visitors to the city following the attacks purchased and wore the shirts bearing the I Love New York logo as a sign of their support. Glaser created a modified version to commemorate the attacks, reading "I ♥ NY MORE THAN EVER," with a little black spot on the heart symbolizing the World Trade Center site. The black spot approximates the site's location on Manhattan Island.

From organic to topological geography, the heart of Manhattan, of world capital, of the world that renders everything and everyone New York: an affect mapped onto a city drawn from the body through the collapse of public and private suffering, the end of history. But who is the "I" here that loves New York? Who speaks this line, this rebus that I wear close to my heart, over my heart? Who is meant to speak? Whose expression of interiority is this? How can this "I" speak itself alone if we are all American?[5]

An elaborate economy traverses the T-shirt, a supplemental memory (souvenir) born of the body: where I have been; where it, my body, has been. From the subject of enunciation ("I") to the unnamed affect seared onto the body that is itself an organ ("♥") to the object or target of the phrase ("NY") to the *objet petit a*, unnamed and perhaps unnamable ("you"), the T-shirt establishes a cryptic passage of the subject through the affective landscape it invokes. The T-shirts function primarily as souvenirs, targeting tourists (and making them targets): the nonnative other (we) loves New York. ("Many visitors to the city following the attacks purchased and wore the shirts bearing the I Love New York logo as a sign of their support." But even before 911, the shirts were destined for the other's body.) The economy of enunciation is worth thinking through to its end. The T-shirt claims that "I," the wearer, loves New York, or rather that the wearer "♥ NY." But the subject of enunciation is still the native New Yorker, who ♥ NY. In purchasing and wearing the shirt, the tourist bears the expression of the New Yorker, serving as a transmitter of the other's affect, an affect-ventriloquist. The T-shirt is the testimony (or *souvenir*) of another's affect: I bear witness that you love New York. The T-shirt effects a citation, made by the tourist, of the New Yorker's unspeakable affection (♥) for New York. The "I" that speaks on and through the T-shirt is not the same as the one who wears the souvenir, who bears the memory of another's affect. The other subject speaks in, on, and through me: "You love New York as me, in my place." I ask you to love (me, NY) as me, in lieu of me: a displaced narcissism and foreign interior. You, the foreigner, visitor, other loves New York. This heart is the other's heart, the other that loves me (I am New York, we are all New Yorkers). We ♥ New York. I ask the other—nonnative, foreigner, tourist, guest, other, intruder, *arrivant*, as Derrida might say—to bear, to wear my sentiment ("I love New York") in my place, in place of me, allowing me to remain in this transaction heartless. This other is me, speaks for me, as me, on behalf of me. I am the other that loves NY: I love the other who and to whom I am.

When I assume (after 911) the T-shirt designed for and designated to the other, I become other, looking in from the outside. (Wearing one's heart on one's sleeve is to expose oneself, one's true thoughts or emotions to another, to everyone.) I wear the other's affect, which is already a displacement of my own expression impressed on the surface of the other. I become the other that stands for me, a *mise-en-abîme* of myself, what Freud calls a target of desire, of my own desire. I am exposed. I am the target of the other's violence and love, but always a missing object, in the psychoanalytic sense, a missing object of desire. My heart is elsewhere, on you, a displaced target. You love NY, where I no longer am, and you suffer in these ruins.[6]

What kind of declaration is made in the form of a rebus, a mixture of pictures and words, symbols and things designed in code to say, in this case, what one truly feels? (An impure language of grafts and transpositions, transplanted signs, an unconscious language and the language of the unconscious. 911, which Derrida calls a "violence without name," is itself such a name, a coded name or cryptonym uttered in an Oriental language of the event [*Philosophy* 113].)[7] What is the status and force of the ♥ in this expression? Is it interchangeable with love, and are the two synonyms—an organ and an affect, a symbol and a concept? Derrida speaks of the heart in Jean-Luc Nancy, of "*his* heart" (*On Touching* 267), one's heart (one's own heart), the other's heart or other heart that Nancy carries in him as an organ and figure.[8] "The heart: absolute intimacy of the limitless secret, no external border, absolute inside, crypt for oneself of an untouchable self-interiority [. . .] inmost core of that which symbolizes the origin of life, within the body, by its displacement of it" (267). It is the place where I am, of absolute intimacy, but where I am absolutely inaccessible to myself: "[T]he heart is never far away," says Derrida, infinitely, endlessly never far away (267).[9] Never far away, like the end itself. It is where everything begins and everything ends, here but never here to me, coming to me from elsewhere. The heart is a limitless limit ("with no external border," "the origin of life" but only in its possible and perhaps eventual "displacement"), absolute singularity here and everywhere. At work in the heart, in the work of the heart, is a paradox: "[T]he heart," says Derrida, "is not only the insensitive figure of the center or of secret interiority; it is the sensible heart, the rhythm, respiration, and beating of the blood, the bloody heart or the bleeding heart" (267).[10] Insensitive, secret, distant, even absent heart; sensual, expressive, tactile "bleeding heart," two hearts beating as one.

Derrida reads the deconstruction of this "absolute intimacy" of the heart in Nancy; the "limitless secret" of the heart is, in Nancy's case, literally and figuratively the secret of another, of the other and the other's heart. It provokes for Nancy and for Derrida the anxiety of one's own propriety, of belonging to oneself, and of *owning* oneself. Of the material heart (as opposed to the figure of "the center, life, *psuchē*, *pneuma*, spirit, interiority, feeling, love"), Derrida says: "It is the body, it is the heart insofar as it is yours belonging to me, the other heart, the heart of the other, there where the 'spiritual' figure, the inherited metonymy, touches this heart, my body, in my body, and can no longer be dissociated from it" (283). The place where figure and organ touch metonymically, where I am me because of you (the heart of the other) and, by extension, you are you because of me, my heart: you carry, wear, bear the heart of the heart of the other (as your own), as I bear yours.

The absolute intimacy achieved in the heart of the heart—origin of life, my life, and the presence of the other, the other's heart—begins not in the figure of the heart, "from the Bible, for example," says Derrida (*On Touching* 283), but in the actual heart, the organ. In "L'Intrus," Nancy situates the originary dilemma of the other's heart, of the other's heart in him:

I have—Who?—this "I" is precisely the question, the old question: what is this enunciating subject? Always foreign to the subject of its own utterance; necessarily intruding upon it, yet ineluctably its motor, shifter, or heart—I, therefore, received the heart of another, now nearly ten years ago. It was a transplant, grafted on. My own heart (as you've gathered, it is entirely a matter of the "proper," of being one, or one's "own"—or else it is not in the least and, properly speaking, there is nothing to understand, no mystery, not even a question: rather, as the doctors prefer to say, there is the simple necessity [la simple évidence] *of a transplantation)—my own heart in fact was worn out, for reasons that have never been clear. Thus to live, it was necessary to receive another's, an other, heart. (3)*

"Always foreign to the subject of its own utterance," the expression (of) "my heart" divides me from my own and its own utterance, from the site of enunciation. In me, in my heart—Nancy's heart, but also all hearts exposed here in the paradox of the heart Derrida describes—the other speaks. But this speaking is not merely a transmission of or possession by the other; it is the other speaking my heart: I see into my heart in the other who speaks it. Who wears it. If the heart is the "crypt for oneself of an untouchable self-interiority," as Derrida says, then Nancy's deconstruction of the heart of the other renders this self-interiority an untouchable self-exteriority or a touchable, detachable, mobile form of interiority that transposes the secret outside, a crypt worn and expressed on the outside. "The heart of this other heart cannot be touched, does not touch *itself,*" says Derrida, "it *self*-touches *you*" (*On Touching* 283). The other speaks cryptically from the ♥.

A crypt or tomb; an end that is not always (or is never) an end, which does not always (or ever) bring closure. (The crypt forms in a parenthesis, suspended from the movement of life but buried alive deep within it, inside and out, within and without.) For Nicolas Abraham and Maria Torok, who challenged the end of the end in the crypt, its finality and finitude, the crypt leaves, in the end and after, a language of the crypt, a cryptic language of cryptonyms (proper names), you and me. The crypt is a cryptonym, a form of language after language, language after the end of language, an aftereffect of language. At the end and after, something always remains but without a common language—the remainder after the end signals the advent of the cryptonym, the secret language of language.

When the dialectic of mourning fails, Abraham and Torok argue, when the process of restoring loss through the process of grieving and normative negativity reach an impasse, when words fail, the subject incorporates the other without integration, producing a useless remainder of the other within the self. (*Within* is a misleading spatial metaphor: the incorporation of the other, of the suspended loss of the other is no more an incorporation than an *excorporation*. The lost object that has entered me, that acts within me as a subject, as a subject of a subject is no less *without* me than within me. The other is there without me within me; I am lost in the other that is lost in me.)[11] The formation of the crypt through incorporation signals, in Abraham and Torok's phantom economy, the end of figurative language. Words become objects, things, signs, codes, numbers, and symbols, but no longer forms of language. "Love," for example, becomes ♥. "*Incorporation*," Abraham and Torok explain, "*entails the fantasmatic destruction of the act by means of which metaphors become possible: the act of putting the original oral void into words*" ("Mourning," 132). Stripped of their figurative value, words revert to things. Pursuing the logic of incorporation to its end, which they chart against the vicissitudes of introjection in the instance of mourning, Abraham and Torok uncover in their speculative psychology a series of things in place of words, secret words and secret others in place of the subject. You in place of me. In their thought, the crypt forms the basis for an unending end (living death or surviving death) that yields its own language, a limitless, secret language of my end: no language at all since it cannot be shared, transposed, transplanted in another. A language for one user; affects fused to words, codes, numerals; signs with no key; alingual. The event of the end of myself in a useless language that remains, that survives me as the remains I have become.

This dead language was the source of a dispute that Agamben chronicles between Kojève and Georges Bataille over the remains of the end of history. In a December 6, 1937, letter that Bataille wrote to Kojève, whose lectures he attended, Bataille protests the characterization of a useless negativity at the end of history. For Kojève, following Hegel, negativity makes history possible, humanity itself possible; at the end of history, either this negativity disappears into a tranquil state of natural harmony—"Man remains alive as animal in *harmony* with Nature or given Being," says Kojève (158)—or it remains without any usefulness as a useless negativity, no longer human but animal. Either way, history ends in some form of animal, animals form the end of history. Agamben adds: "If history is nothing but the patient dialectical work of negation, and man both the subject and the stakes in this negating action, then the completion of history necessarily entails the end of man" (7). But for Bataille, this end does not come at the end (and he claims it does not for Hegel either):

> *If action ("doing") is—as Hegel says—negativity, the question arises as to whether the negativity of one who has "nothing more to do" disappears or remains in a state of "negativity with no use": personally, I can only decide in one way, being myself precisely this "negativity with no use" (I would not be able to define myself more precisely). I recognize that Hegel has foreseen such a possibility; at any rate he didn't situate it at the end of the process he described. I imagine that my life—or better yet, its aborting, the open wound that is my life—constitutes all by itself the refutation of Hegel's closed system. (qtd. in Agamben 7)*

History ends for Hegel when negativity is no longer useful; the end of history is marked by the appearance of a useless negativity. But for Bataille, the useless negativity that he himself claims to be takes place at the center of history, at its heart, and not after its end. It marks an end (a useless negativity) inscribed in the heart of life. It opens (like a wound) Hegel's closed system of the end of history, aborting the end of history before it ends. I am already useless, says Bataille, before the end of history; I am a useless end within history, the end of history transplanted in the heart of history. Although I have reached my end, I do not disappear but remain as a negativity with no use, here now, after the fact, a living end, living on or after the end before the end has come. I survive the end of history and remain after the end as an intrusion, an aborted life or "open wound," he says. A bleeding heart at the end of history, an open wound at the heart of the end of history.

In this open wound that is life, his life, Bataille finds an end in the middle, at the center or origin, in the heart of life. Bataille's open wound prefigures the specter of what Derrida calls the "unimaginable" scene of touching one's own heart, of an "operation of open-heart surgery on oneself" (*On Touching* 267). ("The event, if there is one," says Derrida, "consists in doing the impossible" ["Certain" 231].) Is this not the specter of an aborted life that one continues to live, living on before the end that comes too soon, prematurely, before the end? A ghost or specter that haunts the end before it comes to pass, a phantom before the fact? It signals a secret and intimate end in the middle of life, rendering life (me) useless before the end. This is Bataille's protest against Hegel and Kojève: it is not the end but life itself that produces the remainder, the residual or surplus negativity. To live life, to learn to live life as a useless negativity is the task of art, music, play, and love—and the "poetry, religion, philosophy" it engenders, says Agamben (76)—during life and not after it ends.

But what exactly is this uselessness that Bataille champions and with which he identifies? It is not a question of value; Bataille accepts, it seems, the axioms of Hegel's history that action—negativity—yields both history and humanity. It is the "closed system," the dialectic that ends in the end and generates waste at the end, which Bataille rejects. That is, the end—the useless inhuman and ahistorical negativity—does not take place at the end of history, after its end as a remainder, but in the heart of it. This is the event of the end: I end, history ends, the world ends in the middle, in the heart of life itself. And there is no "poetry, religion, philosophy" that can represent this aborted life: only codes, signals, affects, numbers, limitless secrets borne by the other. Language is here less useless than ineffective and cryptic—an "insensitive figure," as Derrida says of the heart. At the heart of life, of absolute intimacy, is its end, already.

What end then? What end of the event—of history, of humanity—that already takes place, has already taken place, before the end, remaining as a useless negativity—a useless action, a uselessly performative act—before the end, signaling the end of the event before its end? Bataille's protest against Hegel, against Kojève is worth pursuing to its end: "[A]t any rate he didn't situate it at the *end* of the process he described." Following the line of Bataille's thought: useless negativity arrives before the end, not after it; if uselessness defines the end of action, the end of history, the end of humanity, then those conditions have already ended during his lifetime (even Hegel's) and not after, which is to say that history ends *in* history, not at its end. I am this useless negativity embodied, "I would not be able to define myself more precisely." To imagine oneself as a "negativity with no use" as Bataille does, as the living end of history or the specter of the end of history before its time, might also be taken up as the general condition of art, music, play, and love in Bataille's discourse. The useless remainder is a language no longer capable of action in the sense that Hegel and Kojève understand it, but full of the erotic capacity to render from its own uselessness the event of the end: of history, humanity, the world; of you and of me. For Bataille, *eros* is the advent of myself at the moment of my end in the encounter with another; it is the moment of my simultaneous beginning and end. I lose myself in the other (jouissance). *Eros* marks an impossible present, an impossible presence, since I am there and not there (at once), each a condition of my presence at that moment. In Bataille's idiom, the erotic instant (of my end in the other) is the uselessness that makes art possible, that gives birth to art in Lascaux and elsewhere.[12] Bataille's useless end is erotic because it captures the *sense* (and essence) of my limit, my end as a metonymic figure of the end, as an index of my end in you. I am the end, and in the end, you. I end in you, where I survive. It is the collapse of this distinction—you and me, love and hate—the end of an ambivalence that allows life itself, which forms any affective, psychic, and meaningful being in the world, and signals the end of the world as an event. Against the dialectical logic pursued by Hegel and Kojève, which renders negativity productive, Bataille's erotic uselessness produces a remainder with no purpose: it is the birth of myself as object, open wound, artwork. The world is reduced to one, but a one that does not adhere to the protocols of singularity: everything is one, every one a cataclysm, but no one useful. Each is born of the collapse of multiplicity into a catastrophic singularity; or, inversely—and as an extension of the line of catastrophic singularity—an unending catastrophe: a singularity that survives everywhere, in everyone, in the end and as the end before the end.

What remains in the end and after is an affect, the useless rest of an affect no longer proper to me but singular nonetheless, an affect that has overtaken me after my end, which lingers in the space I leave vacant. It is felt, the end, like the immediate sensation of the event after 911, as Derrida says, "the very impact of what is at least *felt*, in an apparently immediate way, to be an event that truly marks, that truly makes its mark, a singular and, as they say here, 'unprecedented' event" (*Philosophy* 86). At the end, I am affected; the end of the world (which always comes before the end, in the middle and at its heart, and which always leaves a remainder) comes to me as a sensation, a perception, a meaning, or a belief of the end of the world, of everything. The world no longer has any meaning to speak of; it no longer discloses meaning in the sense that Martin Heidegger imagines when he says "the world worlds." Or rather, perhaps this is *exactly* what Heidegger has in mind when he claims that the world exceeds "the mere collection of the countable or uncountable, familiar and unfamiliar things that are just there": "Wherever those decisions of our history that relate to our very being are made, are taken up and abandoned by us, go unrecognized and are rediscovered by new inquiry, there the world worlds" (43). The world performs the world, the worldliness of the world in history, in our history. We are in history to the extent that history relates to "our very being," to the extent that as the *world worlds*, meaning is uncovered for and truth is revealed to us—our truths, our meanings (of ourselves), destined for us.

At the end of history, at the end of the world, the meaning that arrives is no longer proper to "us." We are no longer revealed in the world, since we no longer exist in it. The world ends our place in it. Meaning that comes from the world no longer comes to me, but to another, to the other. I sense meaning without understanding it. Meaning takes shape or arrives in the form of an affect. I feel it (as it passes me by, passes through me). At the end of the world, says Nancy, "the world *no longer has a sense*, but it *is* sense" (*Sense* 8). What remains is not a sense of the world, a sensation of or sensibility toward the world—meaning in the world—but the world as sense: "It *is* sense." Meaning has receded from the world, and I can no longer make sense of the world; rather, I sense the world that has become sense, that remains after the end of the world as sense. A feeling of the end of the world, the end of the world in a feeling, a feeling that remains after the end of the world, an after-affect of the end of the world.

The event of the end produces in me, on me, an affect no longer properly my own. It is the world's affect. I am rendered senseless, insensitive to the end, numb to it, a number in it. An affect after the end; a senseless affect or sense of the world's end that is no longer sensible (accessible) to me—an other's affect, another affect. No longer in me but on me, about me, all around me. It is the advent of myself as other—foreign, Oriental—a feeling that returns to me from the outside, after the end, as a senseless *after-affect* of the end of the world. Nothing remains of this event of the end of the world but my heart, worn by another, which is itself in another world and a beginning.

AKIRA MIZUTA LIPPIT is Professor of Cinema, Comparative Literature, and Japanese Culture at the University of Southern California. He is the author of *Electric Animal: Toward a Rhetoric of Wildlife* (University of Minnesota Press, 2000) and *Atomic Light (Shadow Optics)* (University of Minnesota Press, 2005). At present, he is preparing a manuscript on experimental film and video and beginning work on a study of contemporary Japanese cinema.

Notes   1   Giorgio Agamben quotes without commentary the shift in Kojève's discourse regarding the return to animality at the end of history from a state of *happiness* to one of *contentment*. In his 1938–39 lectures, Kojève describes the disappearance of "Man," "Time," and "Philosophy" among other features of History at the end of history; only the World remains "what it has been from all eternity" (158–59). "All the rest," he says, "can be preserved indefinitely; art, love, play, etc., etc., in short everything that makes Man *happy*" (158–59). In a note added to the 1968 edition of *Introduction to the Reading of Hegel*, Kojève revises this thought by renouncing happiness as an effect of the return to natural "art, love, play, etc., etc.," stating that "one cannot say that all this 'makes Man *happy.'* One would have to say post-historical animals of the species *Homo sapiens* (which will live amidst abundance and complete security) will be *content* as a result of their artistic, erotic, and playful behavior, inasmuch as, by definition, they will be contented with it" (159). Content and contented with, satisfied with and made happy by, but also made up of this contentment or happiness. Although Agamben's reading of these passages focuses on the dispute between Kojève and Bataille over the status of the rest or remainder, the useless remainder or "negativity with no use" that rises up from the abyss that ends history, the subtle shift in nuance from happiness, which implies greater agency of affect and a deeper form of remaining animal presence after the end of history, to contentment, which suggests merely a mode of synchronicity with nature, seems to have everything to do with the problem of negativity after history—of a negativity that is, following the Hegelian logic that Kojève extends and Bataille contests, impossible with the collapse of history and the historicity that made negativity possible in the first instance (Agamben 6–9). (Bataille rejects the notion that art, love, and play are rendered useless in the wake of history, which is to say the nostalgic belief that they were once in fact useful. He posits instead that their historical force was always an effect of their uselessness, that he is himself already this "negativity with no use." Bataille suggests in the exchange Agamben cites that he himself embodies a useless negativity that has determined the historicity of history. In this sense, Bataille is a priori useless, useless before the fact, a useless affect that makes possible the end of history *in* history.) In the space

of the useless remainder after history, of the negativity without use or force, emerges a kind of restless affect: happiness or contentment in lieu of action, productive negativity, and the force of history. A horizon of affect opens outward as the aftermath of history, where nothing remains but useless affect. For more on Bataille's relationship to negativity and animality and on Kojève's theses on the return to animality at the end of history, see Lippit.

2   Writing after his 1959 trip to Japan, Kojève speaks of an enduring Japanese "snobbery," one that produces, after the end of history, a mode of formalized survival:

But in spite of persistent economic and social equalities, all Japanese without exception are currently in a position to live according to totally formalized *values—that is, values completely empty of all "human" content in the "historical" sense. Thus, in the extreme, every Japanese is in principle capable of committing, from pure snobbery, a perfectly "gratuitous" suicide (the classical sword of the samurai can be replaced with an airplane or torpedo), which has nothing to do with the* risk *of life in a Struggle waged for the sake of "historical" values that have social or political content. (161–62)*

In Kojève's totalizing view ("all Japanese without exception . . ."), the Japanese die at a distance from themselves, from the samurai sword to the airplane and torpedo. Their lives and deaths are performed, in the theatrical and linguistic senses of the term, at a distance, outside of history—life and death are formalities for the Japanese, executed out of snobbery. Life and death are empty for the nonhistorical Japanese: there are no events of life and death, only their performance.

3   Lloyd Pratt points out that at least two numerical variations appear in the English or American idiom, "nine-eleven" and "nine-one-one," in addition to "September Eleven," and various other euphemisms. Their graphical counterparts also fluctuate between "9–1–1," "911," "9.11," and "9/11," among others. Although the turn to numerical designations invokes significantly the Asian mode of *designating* events by abbreviating and collapsing the dates into clusters of numbers, the indeterminacy underscores first and foremost the quality of an event that escapes naming and even descriptive language itself.

4   The two symbolic limits that frame the Pacific War, Pearl Harbor and Hiroshima, are frequently invoked in relation to 911. The twin towers of the World Trade Center destroyed in the New York attack of September 11, 2001, were designed by Japanese-American architect Minoru Yamasaki; the specter of East Asia—particularly Japan—haunts this event, echoed in the evocations of Pearl Harbor on the one hand, Hiroshima on the other. In a 1998 interview with John Miller of ABC News, Osama bin Laden, accused architect of 911, said:

> *Through history, American [sic] has not been known to differentiate between the military and the civilians or between men and women or adults and children. Those who threw atomic bombs and used the weapons of mass destruction against Nagasaki and Hiroshima were the Americans. Can the bombs differentiate between military and women and infants and children? America has no religion that can deter her from exterminating whole peoples.*

Bin Laden, according to accounts in the press, has referred to 911 as an "American Hiroshima" and has continued in subsequent communications to refer to Hiroshima, forging a discursive link in his rationale between 911 and Hiroshima. The twin referents of Pearl Harbor and Hiroshima form a complex dialectic, putting United States history on two sides of an opposition—victim and aggressor—both framed vis-à-vis the war with Japan.

5   The phrase "We are all Americans" recalls the closing lines of Alain Resnais and Marguerite Duras's *Hiroshima mon amour* (1959), which ends when Emmanuelle Riva and Okada Eiji assume the names of their cities, each named so by the other, the unnamable names of their private and public traumas, "Hiroshima" and "Nevers." Never again, Hiroshima: a phrase or union that never takes place and that characterizes the union itself as impossible.

6   For more on the epistemology of the target, see Weber. Tracking the signifier "target" in the wake of September 11, 2001, and the outbreak of the second Iraq war in 2003, Weber finds in the economy of the term *target* an idiom for thought itself: "'[T]argeting,'" says Weber, "seems inextricable from thinking" (ix).

7   On the impossible name of 911, Derrida says:

> *"To mark a date in history" presupposes, in any case, that "something" comes or happens for the first and last time, "something" that we do not yet really know how to identify, determine, recognize, or analyze but that should remain from here on in unforgettable: an ineffaceable event in the shared archive of a universal calendar, that is, a supposedly universal calendar, for these are—and I want to insist*

on this at the outset—only sup-
positions and presuppositions.
Unrefined and dogmatic, or else
carefully considered, organized,
calculated, strategic—or all of
these at once. For the index point-
ing toward this date, the bare act,
the minimal deictic, the minimal-
ist aim of this dating, also marks
something else. Namely, the fact
that we perhaps have no concept
and no meaning available to us
to name in any other way this
"thing" that has just happened,
this supposed "event." An act of
"international terrorism," for
example, and we will return to
this, is anything but a rigorous
concept that would help us grasp
the singularity of what we will
be trying to discuss. "Something"
took place, we have the feeling of
not having seen it coming, and
certain consequences undeniably
follow upon the "thing." But this
very thing, the place and meaning
of this "event," remains ineffable,
like an intuition without concept,
like a unicity with no generality
on the horizon or with no horizon
at all, out of range for a language
that admits its powerlessness
and so is reduced to pronouncing
mechanically a date, repeating
it endlessly, as a kind of ritual
incantation, a conjuring poem, a
journalistic litany or rhetorical
refrain that admits to not know-
ing what it's talking about. We
do not in fact know what we are
saying or naming in this way:
September 11, le 11 septembre,
September 11. The brevity of the
appellation (September 11, 9/11)
stems not only from an economic
or rhetorical necessity. The tele-
gram of this metonymy—a name,
a number—points out the unquali-
fiable by recognizing that we do
not recognize or even cognize that
we do not yet know how to qualify,
that we do not know what we are
talking about. (Philosophy 86)
Noam Chomksy, among others,

has frequently pointed out that September 11, 2001, is the *second* 911. The first took place on September 11, 1973, when a United States–backed coup d'état overthrew the government of democratically elected president Salvador Allende Gossens and installed the military dictatorship of General Augusto Pinochet Ugarte. The violent coup involved the bombing of the presidential palace with Allende inside. Two 911s, each singular, although the first 911 has received its name posthumously after the second 911, after the fact and as an aftereffect of the second 911, underscoring the first 911 as an event that has not yet reached its end.

8   Jean-Luc Nancy has lived for almost twenty years with a transplanted heart.

9   "The heart is one of those interior surfaces of the body that, in principle (unless one performs the unimaginable, at least for now, operation of open-heart surgery on oneself), no 'self-touching' can ever reach—what might be termed the heart's hide" (*On Touching* 267). The unimaginable: touching one's own heart, being touched by oneself or an auto-affection.

10 Derrida says more about secrecy and the event, about the secrecy of the event: "The secret belongs to the structure of the event. Not the secret in the sense of something private, clandestine, or hidden, but the secret as that which doesn't appear" ("Certain" 239).

11 There is much more to say but no words left to say it. See Abraham and Torok, *Wolf*.

12 Lascaux is, for Bataille, the scene of the birth of history, rendered and performed in the cave. See Bataille, *Lascaux* and *Tears*.

Works Cited   Abraham, Nicolas, and Maria Torok. "Mourning *or* Melancholia: Introjection *versus* Incorporation." *The Shell and the Kernel.* Ed. and trans. Nicholas T. Rand. Chicago: U of Chicago P, 1994. 125–38.

─────────. *The Wolf Man's Magic Word: A Cryptonymy.* Trans. Nicholas T. Rand. Minneapolis: U of Minnesota P, 1986.

Agamben, Giorgio. *The Open: Man and Animal.* Trans. Kevin Attell. Stanford: Stanford UP, 2004.

Bald, Sunil. "Memories, Ghosts, and Scars: Architecture and Trauma in New York and Hiroshima." *Review of Japanese Culture and Society* 12 (2001): 51–57.

Bataille, Georges. *Lascaux, or the Birth of Art.* Trans. Austryn Wainhouse. Geneva: Skira, 1955.

─────────. *The Tears of Eros.* Trans. Peter Connor. San Francisco: City Lights, 1989.

Derrida, Jacques. "A Certain Impossible Possibility of Saying the Event." *The Late Derrida.* Ed. W. J. T. Mitchell and Arnold I. Davidson. Trans. Gila Walker. Chicago: U of Chicago P, 2007. 223–43.

─────────. *On Touching—Jean-Luc Nancy.* Trans. Christine Irizarry. Stanford: Stanford UP, 2005.

─────────. *Philosophy in a Time of Terror: Dialogues with Jürgen Habermas and Jacques Derrida.* Ed. Giovanna Borradori. Chicago: U of Chicago P, 2004.

DeSouza, D'nesh. *The End of Racism: Principles for a Multiracial Society.* New York: Free Press, 1995.

Heidegger, Martin. "The Origin of the Work of Art." *Poetry, Language, Thought.* Trans. Albert Hofstander. New York: Harper and Row, 1971. 17–86.

Kojève, Alexandre. *Introduction to the Reading of Hegel.* Ed. Allan Bloom. Trans. James H. Nichols, Jr. Ithaca: Cornell UP, 1980.

Lippit, Akira Mizuta. *Electric Animal: Toward a Rhetoric of Wildlife.* Minneapolis: U of Minneapolis P, 2000.

Miller, John. "Interview with Osama bin Laden." 1998. Posted on Frontline, PBS. www.pbs .org/wgbh/pages/frontline/shows/binladen/who/interview.html (accessed May 20, 2008).

Nancy, Jean-Luc. "L'Intrus." Trans. Susan Hanson. CR: *The New Centennial Review* 2.3 (2002): 1–14.

─────────. *The Sense of the World.* Trans. Jeffrey S. Librett. Minneapolis: U of Minnesota P, 1997.

Weber, Samuel. *Targets of Opportunity: On the Militarization of Thinking.* New York: Fordham UP, 2005.